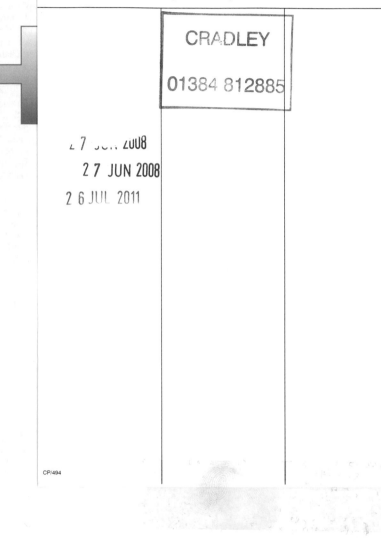

H ay

Tim Falla
Liz and John Soars

OXFORD
UNIVERSITY PRESS

OXFORD
UNIVERSITY PRESS

Great Clarendon Street, Oxford OX2 6DP

Oxford University Press is a department of the University of Oxford.
It furthers the University's objective of excellence in research, scholarship,
and education by publishing worldwide in

Oxford New York

Auckland Cape Town Dar es Salaam Hong Kong Karachi
Kuala Lumpur Madrid Melbourne Mexico City Nairobi
New Delhi Shanghai Taipei Toronto

With offices in

Argentina Austria Brazil Chile Czech Republic France Greece
Guatemala Hungary Italy Japan Poland Portugal Singapore
South Korea Switzerland Thailand Turkey Ukraine Vietnam

OXFORD and OXFORD ENGLISH are registered trade marks of
Oxford University Press in the UK and in certain other countries

© Oxford University Press 2002

The moral rights of the author have been asserted

Database right Oxford University Press (maker)

First published 2002

2009 2008 2007
20 19 18 17 16 15 14 13 12 11

ISBN-13: 978 0 19 437632 7

Printed in China

ACKNOWLEDGEMENTS

Illustrations by:
Adrian Barclay pp10, 11, 22, 31, 48, 49, 72; Josephine Blake p50; Stan Chow
pp33, 75, 76 (Mike & Carol); Paul Daviz pp20, 40, 41, 53, 79; Emma Dodd
pp19, 43, 57, 64-65, 73; Melvyn Evans pp26, 38, 39, 60; Gavin Reece pp12,
62; Harry Venning pp27, 66, 74, 76 (cold, hot…); Mark Watkinson pp7, 9,
44, 46, 47, 68, 78

*The publishers would like to thank the following for their kind permission
to reproduce photographs:*
Action-Plus p8 (N.Tingle/Number 1); Courtesy of Channel 4 p8 (Number
4); Corbis pp8 (Eye Ubiquitous/Number 8), 16 (Fotographica/taxi), 51
(C.Hellier/Shakespeare), (Archico Iconographico S.A./Mozart), 52
(Bettmann), 60 (V.Streano/Tuscany); Digital Vision p80 (zebra); EyeWire p5
(supermarket); Frank Spooner Pictures p21 (Prince Charles & Princess
Anne); GettyOne Image Bank pp16 (Barros & Barros/nurse), 23 (N.Brown);
GettyOne Stone pp5 (T.Vine/two men shaking hands), 13 (Govin-
Sorel/Roberto), (D.Stewart/Brigitte & Jean-Claude), (A.Sacks/Yumi), 15
(W.Hodges/taxi driver), (D.Day/teacher), (D.Young Wolff/shop assistant),
(J.Brooks/student), 16 (B.Handelman/student), (H.Kingsworth/Rosalinda),
18 (H.Camille/Kirsty), 28 (P.Mason/Xavier & Jorge), 29 (T.Bown/man and
woman), (D.H.Stewart/group), 35 (F.Orel), 40 (R.Charity), 42 (E.Pritchard),
58 (C.Henderson), 61 (D.Durfee), 70 (D.Roth/Jake), (J.Darell/Helga), 71
(B.Ayres/Mitsuo), (V.C.L./Serena); ImageState p30 (J.Magg/from Brazil),
(Masterfile/from Germany, Japan and France), (M.Irving/from Spain),
(Shoot Photography/from Italy); PhotoDisc pp15 (businessman),
(K.Brofsky/nurse), (S.Cole/nurse), 55 (C Squared Studios), 68
(D.Menuez/waiter); Pictor International pp5 (man and woman shaking
hands), (3 people greeting), 8 (Number 10), 15 (doctor), 16 (man at desk),
18 (basketball players), 34, 47, 79 (Amsterdam), (the Smiths), 80 (tour bus);
Popperfoto p25 (Reuters NewMedia Inc); Rex Features pp15 (Alison
Regan/The Sun/policewoman), 21 (T.Rooke/H.R.H.The Queen), (Prince
Philip), (C.Sykes/Prince Andrew), 21 (T.Rooke/Prince Edward), 80 (children
looking at bee); Courtesy of the Science Museum, London, Press Office p80
(child and adult), (child building bridge)

Commissioned photography by:
Gareth Boden pp6, 13 (Henri and Isabel and Anna); Rob Judges pp8
(Numbers 2, 6 and 7), 14

CONTENTS

You will need to listen to the cassette for some exercises. If you don't have the cassette, you can read the tapescripts on pp81–83.

1

What's your name? • What's this in English?
Numbers 1–10 and plurals

What's your name?

1 Put the sentences in the correct order.

1. ☐ My name's Claudia.
   ☐ Hello, Claudia.
   ☐1 Hello. I'm Jean. What's your name?

2. ☐ Fine, thanks.
   ☐ Hi, Massimo. How are you?
   ☐1 Hello, Petra.
   ☐ Very well, thanks. And you?

2 Put the words in the correct order.

1. you / How / are / ?
   How are you?

2. thanks / Very / well
   _____

3. James / is / This
   _____

4. name / What's / your / ?
   _____

5. name's / Raquel / My
   _____

3 **T 1.1** Listen. Match the conversations and photos.

Conversation	1	2	3	4
Photo	d			

4 **T 1.2** Complete the conversations.

1 **Pierre Dupont**   Hello. My **name's** Pierre
                        Dupont. What's your _____ ?

    Alicia González   Alicia. Alicia González.

2 **Pierre**   Hello, Alicia. _____ are you?

   Alicia   _____ , thanks. And _____ ?

   Pierre   Very _____ , _____ .

3 **Alicia**   Pierre, this is Aya Saito. Aya,
               _____ _____ Pierre
               Dupont.

   Aya Saito   Hello, Pierre.

   Pierre   _____ , Aya.

5 Write the conversations.

1 **Klaus Fischer**   Hello. My name's _____
                             _____

   Denise Minjon   _____

2 **Denise**   Hello, Klaus. _____
                      _____

   Klaus   _____

   Denise   _____

3 **Klaus**   _____
                _____

   Paolo Silvetti   _____

   Denise   _____

What's this in English?

6 **T 1.3** Listen and repeat.

> a bag   a book   a camera   a car   a computer   a hamburger
> a house   a photograph   a sandwich   a television

7 Write sentences.

1 *It's a photograph.*   2 _____   3 _____

4 _____   5 _____   6 _____   7 _____

8 _____   9 _____   10 _____

Translation

8 Write the sentences in your language.

1 How are you?   _____

2 Fine, thanks. And you?   _____

3 What's your name?   _____

4 My name's David.   _____

5 What's this?   _____

6 It's a book.   _____

Everyday English

Numbers 1–10 and plurals

9 Write the numbers.

1 *eight*

2 _____

3 _____

4 _____

5 _____

6 _____

7 _____

8 _____

9 _____

10 _____ _____ _____

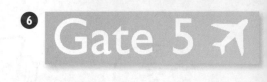

10 **T 1.4** Write the numbers.

1	three	*3*	6	eight	_____
2	five	_____	7	six	_____
3	nine	_____	8	four	_____
4	one	_____	9	seven	_____
5	two	_____	10	ten	_____

11 **T 1.5** Listen. Write the numbers.

1	*6*		5	_____
2	_____		6	_____
3	_____		7	_____
4	_____		8	_____

12 **T 1.6** Write *s* or *es*.

1 car**s**   3 computer___   5 sandwich___   7 photograph___   9 house___

2 camera___   4 book___   6 bag___   8 television___   10 hamburger___

13 Write numbers and words.

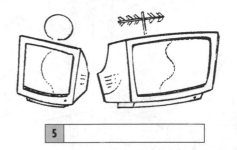

1	five cars

2	

3	

4	

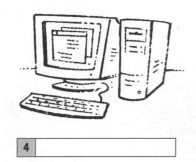

5	

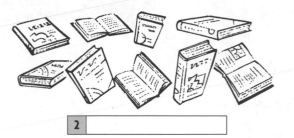

6	

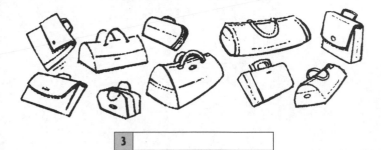

7	

8	

9	

10	

Countries • Where are you from? • *he/she, his/her;*
I/you , my/your • Numbers 11–30

Your world

Countries

1 What are the countries? Write *a, e, i, o,* and *u.*

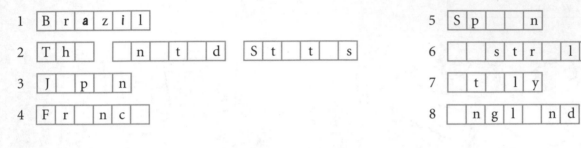

1 | B | r | **a** | z | **i** | l |

2 | T | h | | | n | t | d | | S | t | | t | | s |

3 | J | | p | | n |

4 | F | r | | n | c | |

5 | S | p | | | n |

6 | | | s | t | r | | l | | |

7 | | t | | l | y |

8 | | n | g | l | | n | d |

2 Write the countries.

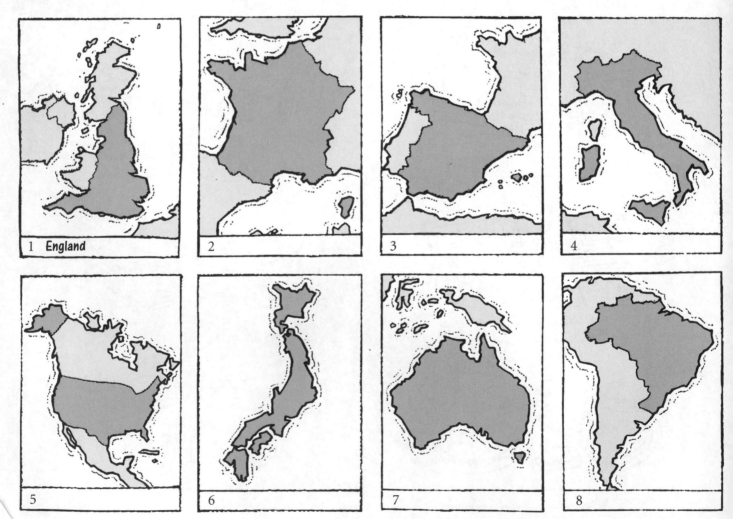

1 **England**

2

3

4

5

6

7

8

Pronunciation

3 **T 2.1** Put these countries into the correct columns, A, B, C, D, or E.

> England ~~Brazil~~ Australia
> ~~Spain~~ Japan France Italy

A ●	B ●●	C ●●	D ●●●	E ●●●●
<u>Spain</u> _____	_____	<u>Brazil</u> _____	_____	_____

Cities and countries

4 Write questions and answers.

> ~~Barcelona~~ Boston Oxford Milan
> Paris Rio de Janeiro Sydney Tokyo

1 **A** <u>Where's Barcelona?</u>

   B <u>It's in Spain.</u>

2 **A** _____

   B _____

3 **A** _____

   B _____

4 **A** _____

   B _____

5 **A** _____

   B _____

6 **A** _____

   B _____

7 **A** _____

   B _____

8 **A** _____

   B _____

5 **T 2.2** Write the countries.

> England Scotland Wales
> ~~Northern Ireland~~

1 <u>Northern Ireland</u>

2 _____

3 _____

4 _____

Where are you from?

he/she, his/her

6 **T 2.3** Write questions and answers.

1 **A** What's <u>his</u> name?
  B His name's <u>Gianni</u> .
  A Where's <u>he</u> from?
  B He's from <u>Italy</u>.

4 **A** _____ name?
  B _____
  A _____ from?
  B _____ from _____ .

2 **A** What's _____ name?
  B Her name's _____ .
  A Where's _____ from?
  B She's from _____ .

5 **A** _____ name?
  B _____
  A _____
  B _____

3 **A** What's _____ name?
  B His name's _____ .
  A Where's _____ from?
  B He's from _____ .

6 **A** _____
  B _____
  A _____
  B _____

I/you, my/your

7 Complete the conversations.

1 **Henri** Hello. My name's Henri. **What's**
   _____ name?

   Isabel Isabel.

   Henri Where _____ you _____ ,
   Isabel?

   Isabel Coimbra, in Portugal. Where
   _____ _____ from?

   Henri _____ from Paris.

2 **Henri** _____ , Isabel. _____ are you?

   Isabel _____ , thanks. And _____ ?

   Henri Very well, _____ . Isabel, _____ is
   Ana. _____ _____ Portugal.

   Isabel _____ , Ana.

   Ana _____ , Isabel. _____ are you
   _____ ?

   Isabel _____ _____ Coimbra.

   Ana Oh, _____ _____ Coimbra,
   _____ !

Reading

They're from ...

8 **T 2.4** Read and listen.

This is Roberto. He's
in Sydney. He's from
Italy. He's a computer
programmer.

This is Brigitte and
Jean-Claude. They're
married and they're
from France. Brigitte
is a teacher and
Jean-Claude is a
photographer.

This is a photograph of
Yumi. She's from Japan.
She's a doctor. Her
hospital is in the centre
of Tokyo.

9 Complete the sentences.

1 Roberto is in **Sydney** .

2 He's from _____ .

3 He's a _____ .

4 Brigitte and Jean-Claude are _____ .

5 They're from _____ .

6 Brigitte is a _____ .

7 _____ is a photographer.

8 Yumi is from _____ .

9 She's a _____ .

10 Her _____ is in the centre of Tokyo.

Listening

This is Carmen

10 **T 2.5** Look at the photograph and listen. Choose the correct answers.

1 Carmen is (a doctor) / a teacher.

2 *She's in* / *She's from* Madrid.

3 This is a photograph of *her house* / *her school*.

4 Her school is in the centre of *Liverpool* / *London*.

5 Her teacher is *Andrew* / *Anthony*.

6 He's from *England* / *Scotland*.

Translation

11 **Write the sentences in your language.**

1 Where are you from?

_____

2 I'm from Brazil.

_____

3 Where's Eduardo from?

_____

4 He's from Spain.

_____

5 They're from the United States.

_____

6 Her name is Susan. His name is Mike.

_____

Everyday English

Numbers 11–30

12 **T 2.6** Listen and repeat.

11	12	13	14	15	16	17	18	19	20
21	22	23	24	25	26	27	28	29	30

13 Match the numbers and words.

> twelve   23   eighteen   22   twenty-eight   16
>
> twenty-one   25   fifteen   13   nineteen   12
>
> 18   twenty-nine   15   thirty   11   twenty   27
>
> seventeen   20   fourteen   26   sixteen   21
>
> 29   twenty-seven   14   twenty-three   24
>
> twenty-two   17   twenty-four   28   eleven
>
> twenty-five   19   twenty-six   30   thirteen

14 Write the numbers.

1 13 thirteen   6 17 _____
2 29 _____   7 11 _____
3 12 _____   8 30 _____
4 15 _____   9 27 _____
5 20 _____   10 21 _____

15 Write the numbers.

1 11 + 11 = twenty-two   6 4 × 4 = _____
2 7 × 4 = _____   7 3 × 8 = _____
3 3 × 6 = _____   8 20 − 1 = _____
4 7 + 6 = _____   9 13 + 13 = _____
5 30 − 7 = _____   10 5 × 5 = _____

16 **T 2.7** Listen. Write the numbers.

1 16   6 _____
2 _____   7 _____
3 _____   8 _____
4 _____   9 _____
5 _____   10 _____

3

Jobs • Negatives – *isn't* • Address, phone number ...
What's your job? • Social expressions

Personal information

Jobs

1 **T 3.1** What are the jobs? Write *a, e, i, o,* and *u.*

1 | t | a | x | i | | d | r | i | v | e | r |

2 | b | | s | | n | | s | s | m | | n |

3 | d | | c | t | | r |

4 | n | | r | s | e |

5 | p | | l | | c | | | | f | f | | c | | r |

6 | s | h | | p | | | s | s | | s | t | | n | t |

7 | s | t | | d | | n | t |

8 | t | | | c | h | | r |

2 **T 3.2** Write questions and answers.

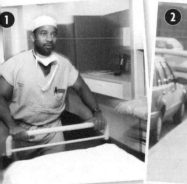
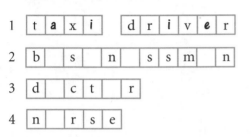

1 A *What's his job?*
  B *He's a nurse.*

2 A *What's her job?*
  B *She's a police officer.*

3 A _____
  B _____

4 A _____
  B _____

5 A _____
  B _____

6 A _____
  B _____

7 A _____
  B _____

8 A _____
  B _____

15

Unit 3 · Personal information   15

Negatives – *isn't*

3 [T 3.3] Write sentences with *is* and *isn't*.

he / student ✗ / teacher ✔

1   **He isn't a student.**
    He's a teacher.

she / doctor ✗ / nurse ✔

2   _____
    _____

he / businessman ✗ / police officer ✔

3   _____
    _____

she / taxi driver ✗ / shop assistant ✔

4   _____
    _____

Address, phone number . . .

4 Write the words on the identity card.

Address	Age	Country	Job
Married?	Phone number	~~Name~~	

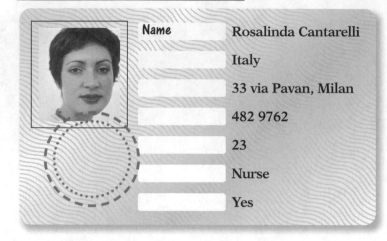

Name Rosalinda Cantarelli

_____ Italy

_____ 33 via Pavan, Milan

_____ 482 9762

_____ 23

_____ Nurse

_____ Yes

Questions and short answers

5 Write the questions.

1   **What's her name?**
    Rosalinda Cantarelli.

2   _____ ?
    Italy.

3   _____ ?
    33 via Pavan, Milan.

4   _____ ?
    482 9762.

5   _____ ?
    She's 23.

6   _____ ?
    She's a nurse.

7   _____ ?
    Yes, she is.

6 Answer these questions about Rosalinda Cantarelli.
Use short answers.

1   Is Rosalinda from the United States?
    No, she isn't.

2   Is she from France?
    _____

3   Is she from Italy?
    _____

4   Is she 22?
    _____

5   Is she 23?
    _____

6   Is she a shop assistant?
    _____

7   Is she a nurse?
    _____

8   Is she married?
    _____

What's your job?

Questions and short answers

7 **T 3.4** Answer the questions about <u>you</u>. Write short answers.

1 Are you Tom Walker?

_____

2 Are you from Rome?

_____

3 Are you a student?

_____

4 Are you 24?

_____

5 Are you married?

_____

8 Write questions. Put the words in the correct order.

1 your / what's / name / ?
   What's your name?

2 are / where / from / you / ?

_____

3 address / your / what's / ?

_____

4 your / what's / number / phone / ?

_____

5 are / you / how / old / ?

_____

6 what's / job / your / ?

_____

7 married / you / are / ?

_____

9 Now answer the questions in exercise 8. Answer about <u>you</u>.

1 **My name is** _____

2 _____

3 _____

4 _____

5 _____

6 _____

7 _____

Translation

10 Write the sentences in your language.

1 I'm not married.

_____

2 What's your job?

_____

3 'Is James from Scotland?' 'No, he isn't.'

_____

4 'How old is she?' 'She's twenty-six.'

_____

5 Sonya and Paul aren't from France.

_____

Pronunciation

11 **T 3.5** Listen and repeat.

●	●●	●●●
Spain	seven	Italy
thanks	camera	photograph

12 **T 3.6** Put the words into the correct columns, A, B, or C.

~~book~~ car doctor fine student hospital number nurse officer Portugal sandwich hamburger

A ●	B ●●	C ●●●
book	_____	_____
_____	_____	_____
_____	_____	_____
_____	_____	_____

Listening

A conversation with Kirsty

13 **T 3.7** Listen to the conversation. Complete the information.

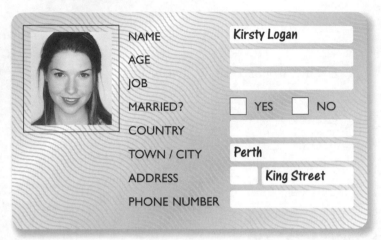

NAME	**Kirsty Logan**
AGE	
JOB	
MARRIED?	☐ YES ☐ NO
COUNTRY	
TOWN / CITY	**Perth**
ADDRESS	**King Street**
PHONE NUMBER	

14 Answer the questions about Kirsty. Use short answers.

1 Is Kirsty 25?

   No, she isn't.

2 Is Kirsty a student?

   _____

3 Is she a shop assistant?

   _____

4 Is she married?

   _____

5 Is she from Scotland?

   _____

6 Is she from Edinburgh?

   _____

7 Is her phone number 417 8524?

   _____

Reading

An international team

15 **T 3.8** Read and listen to the interview. Answer the questions.

Interviewer	This is Paul, Ashley, Michael, and Carlos. They're basketball players. Now, you're American, aren't you?
Ashley	Well, Paul and I are American. But, er, Carlos and Michael aren't.
Michael	No, I'm not American. I'm from Canada. And Carlos is from Cuba.
Interviewer	Uh, huh. An international team! And you're on tour in England.
Ashley	That's right. We're at the London Arena.
Michael	London's great!
Interviewer	Good. Now, how old are you?
Paul	I'm 21. Ashley and Michael are 22.
Carlos	And I'm 24.
Interviewer	OK. Thanks! And welcome to England!

1 Where are Paul and Ashley from?

   _____

2 Are Michael and Carlos American?

   _____

3 Where are they now?

   _____

4 How old are Ashley and Michael?

   _____

5 Is Carlos 21?

   _____

Everyday English

Social expressions

16 **T 3.9** Write the expressions.

> ~~Goodbye~~   Good afternoon   Good night
> Good evening   Good morning

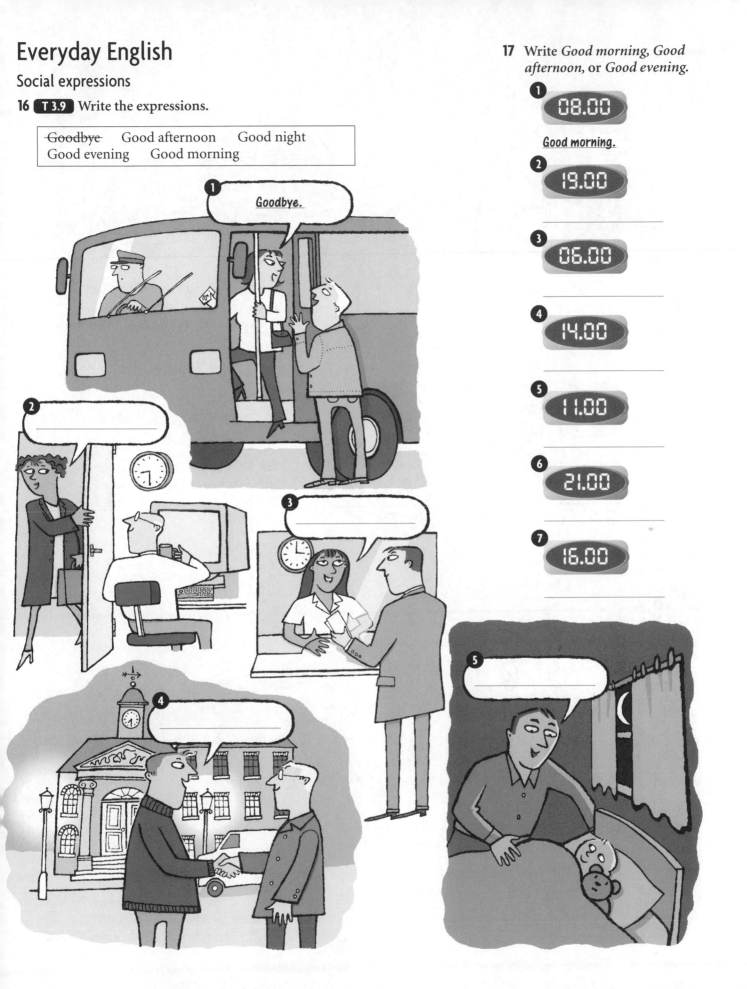

17 Write *Good morning*, *Good afternoon*, or *Good evening*.

1 `08.00`
Good morning.

2 `19.00`

3 `06.00`

4 `14.00`

5 `11.00`

6 `21.00`

7 `16.00`

18 Choose the correct expressions.

1 **Woman** Are you (all right) / sorry?
  Man Yes, I'm OK, thanks.

2 **Student** What's this in English?
  Teacher It's a computer.
  Student *Oh, all right. / Oh, thanks.*

3 **Teacher** Please read the sentences.
  Student *I don't know. / Pardon?*
  Teacher Please read the sentences.
  Student OK.

4 **Woman** *Sorry! / Pardon?*
  Man No problem. It's only water.

5 **Man** Where's Marek from?
  Woman *I don't know. / I don't understand.* Is he from Poland?

4

The family • Possessive **'s** • Possessive adjectives
has/have • The alphabet • On the phone

Family and friends

The family

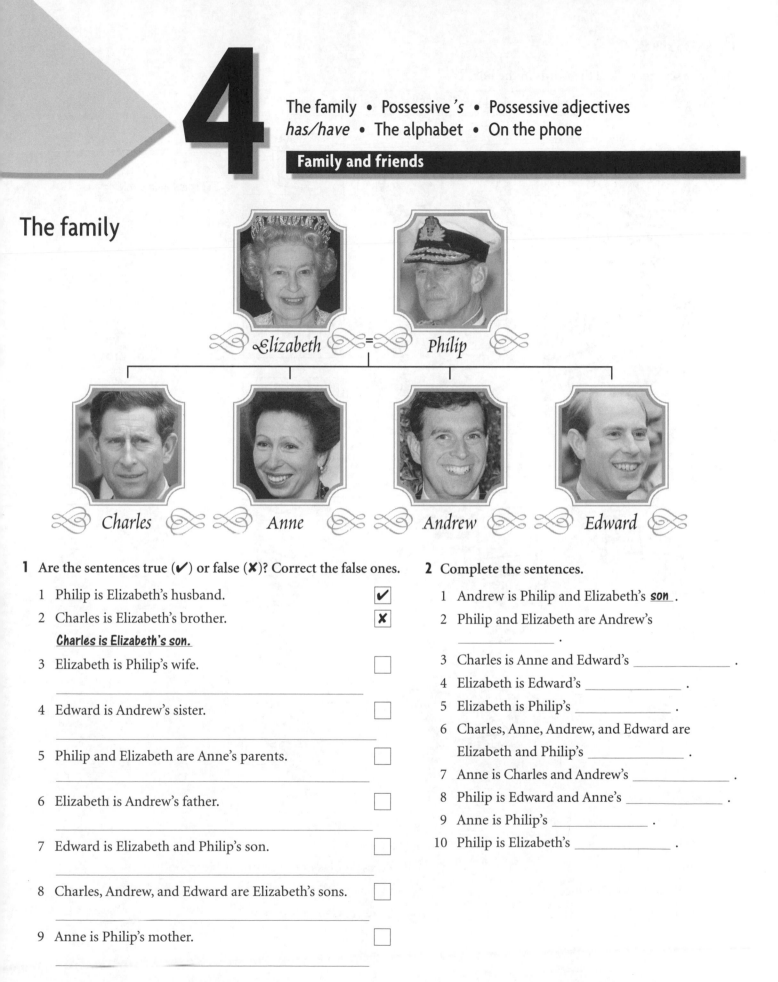

Elizabeth = Philip

Charles   Anne   Andrew   Edward

1 Are the sentences true (✔) or false (✘)? Correct the false ones.

1 Philip is Elizabeth's husband. ✔

2 Charles is Elizabeth's brother. ✘
   Charles is Elizabeth's son.

3 Elizabeth is Philip's wife. ☐
   _____

4 Edward is Andrew's sister. ☐
   _____

5 Philip and Elizabeth are Anne's parents. ☐
   _____

6 Elizabeth is Andrew's father. ☐
   _____

7 Edward is Elizabeth and Philip's son. ☐
   _____

8 Charles, Andrew, and Edward are Elizabeth's sons. ☐
   _____

9 Anne is Philip's mother. ☐
   _____

2 Complete the sentences.

1 Andrew is Philip and Elizabeth's **son** .

2 Philip and Elizabeth are Andrew's
   _____ .

3 Charles is Anne and Edward's _____ .

4 Elizabeth is Edward's _____ .

5 Elizabeth is Philip's _____ .

6 Charles, Anne, Andrew, and Edward are
   Elizabeth and Philip's _____ .

7 Anne is Charles and Andrew's _____ .

8 Philip is Edward and Anne's _____ .

9 Anne is Philip's _____ .

10 Philip is Elizabeth's _____ .

Possessive 's

3 Make sentences. Use the words in the box.

| bag | camera | car | computer | dictionary | dog | house | ~~television~~ |

1 _This is Paolo's television._

2 _____

3 _____

4 _____

5 _____

6 _____

7 _____

8 _____

4 **T 4.1** Write *P* if *'s* = possession. Write *is* if *'s* = *is*.

1 He**'s** a businessman. **is**

2 This is Henri**'s** sister. **P**

3 What**'s** his job? ___

4 William is Peter**'s** father. ___

5 Angela**'s** father is a taxi driver. ___

6 Who**'s** Pedro? ___

7 Maria**'s** 35. ___

8 Jane**'s** school is in the centre of Liverpool. ___

9 Tony**'s** wife is 34. ___

10 Where are George**'s** parents? ___

5 Add *s*, *'s*, or ✗.

1 My name **'s** Pilar.

2 Cathy and Liam are doctor**s** .

3 My parents ✗ are in Germany.

4 What__ your address?

5 This is the teacher__ book.

6 They are police officer__.

7 Where is Vicky__ bag?

8 Her name__ Paula.

9 Their sons__ are Mark and Harry.

10 Her husband__ name is Antonio.

Possessive adjectives

6 Write the possessive adjectives.

Subject pronouns	Possessive adjectives
I	my
you	_____
he	_____
she	_____
we	_____
they	_____

7 Complete the sentences with a possessive adjective.

1 We're from Scotland. **Our** house is in Glasgow.

2 'What's _____ job?' 'I'm a nurse.'

3 'What are _____ names?' 'She's Sonia and he's Olivier.'

4 This is my daughter. _____ name's Victoria.

5 I'm married. _____ wife's Italian.

6 'My brother, John, is in London.' 'Oh, what's _____ address?'

7 Jane and I are doctors. _____ hospital is in Manchester.

Listening

Winston's family

8 **T 4.2** Listen to Winston. Choose the correct answers.

1 Winston is *20* / ⟨*30*⟩.

2 Winston is a *restaurant manager* / *bank manager*.

3 Winston's wife's name is *Carol* / *Karen*.

4 She's *25* / *29*.

5 She's a *nurse* / *teacher*.

6 Jessica is *5* / *6*.

7 Their children are at *school* / *university*.

8 Carol's father is a *shop assistant* / *police officer*.

Vocabulary

Jobs, countries, numbers, families

9 **T 4.3** Put the words into the correct columns.

> ~~Australia~~ Brazil doctor father nineteen
> Japan wife nurse twelve six son Spain
> businessman sister twenty-three teacher

Jobs	Countries
_____	Australia
_____	_____
_____	_____
_____	_____

Numbers	Families
_____	_____
_____	_____
_____	_____
_____	_____

Pronunciation

10 **T 4.4** Listen and repeat.

●	●●	●●	●●●
house	married	Japan	photograph

11 **T 4.5** Put the words into the correct columns, A, B, C, or D.

> ~~address~~ Brazil son hello wife
> daughter family France children
> businessman husband manager

A ●	B ●●	C ●●	D ●●●
_____	_____	address	_____
_____	_____	_____	_____

has/have

12 Write six true sentences about you, your family, and your friends. Use the words in the box.

> ~~a German car~~ a brother a computer
> a dictionary a dog a job a house
> an English teacher a husband a wife
> ~~a Japanese TV~~ a sister two children

1 <u>My brother has a German car.</u>

2 <u>I have a Japanese TV.</u>

3 _____

4 _____

5 _____

6 _____

7 _____

8 _____

13 Complete the sentences. Use *has* and *have*.

1 Paul **has** two brothers.

2 We _____ two dogs.

3 You _____ an Italian name.

4 She _____ a good dictionary.

5 This book _____ 80 pages.

6 I _____ a computer.

7 My daughter _____ a house in London.

Translation

14 Write the sentences in your language.

1 Michael is Beate's husband.

_____

2 What's your sister's phone number?

_____

3 My son has a good job.

_____

4 My parents have a house in France.

_____

5 I have two children.

_____

Reading

15 Read the text and answer the questions.

Michael Douglas and Catherine Zeta-Jones

This is a photo of Michael Douglas and his wife. Michael is from the United States. He's fifty-seven and he's married to Catherine Zeta-Jones. She's thirty-two and she's from Wales. They're both actors. They have one child. Their son's name is Dylan. He's two. Michael and Catherine have the same birthday – 25th September.

1 Where's Michael Douglas from?
He's from the United States.

2 How old is he?
_____

3 What's his wife's name?
_____

4 Where's she from?
_____

5 What are their jobs?
_____

6 What's their son's name?
_____

7 How old is he?
_____

8 When's Michael and Catherine's birthday?
_____

Everyday English

The alphabet

16 **T 4.6** Put the letters into the correct columns.

a	b	c	d	e	f	g	h	i	j	k	l	m
n	o	p	q	r	s	t	u	v	w	x	y	z

/eɪ/	/iː/	/e/	/aɪ/	/əʊ/	/uː/	/ɑː/
<u>a</u>	<u>b</u>	<u>f</u>	<u>i</u>	<u>o</u>	<u>q</u>	<u>r</u>
—	—	—	—	—	—	—
—		—				
		—				
		—				
		—				
		—				

17 **T 4.7** Listen. Write the words.

1 <u>teacher</u>   5 _____
2 _____   6 _____
3 _____   7 _____
4 _____

On the phone

18 **T 4.8** Put the lines in the correct place in the conversation.

> And your name is?
> ~~Good morning. Bath English Language Centre.~~
> How do you spell your surname?
> Thank you for telephoning. Goodbye.
> Thank you. I'm sorry. He isn't in his office.
>   What's your phone number?

A (1) <u>Good morning. Bath English Language Centre.</u>

B Hello. The director, Mike Stevens, please.

A (2) _____

B Akemi Ishikawa.

A (3) _____

B I-S-H-I-K-A-W-A.

A (4) _____
_____

B 813 5824 9687.

A (5) _____

B Goodbye.

Sports, food, and drinks • Present Simple – *I/you/they,* questions and answers • Languages and nationalities Numbers and prices

It's my life!

Sports, food, and drinks

1 **T 5.1** Complete the words.

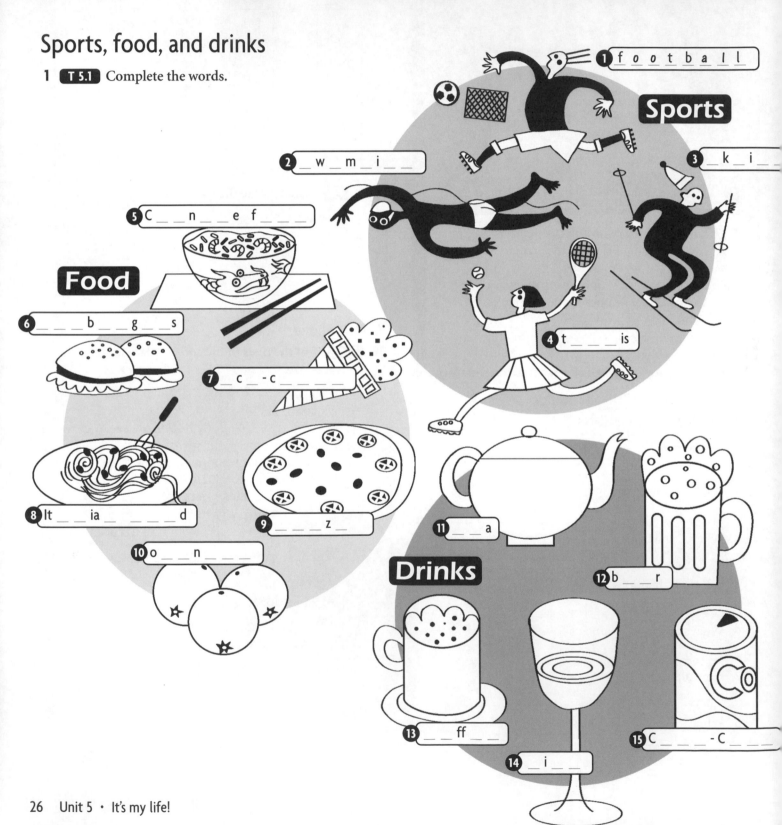

Sports

1 f o o t b a l l

2 _ w _ m _ i _ _ _

3 _ k _ i _ _

4 t _ _ _ _ is

Food

5 C _ _ n _ _ e f _ _ _ _

6 _ _ _ _ b _ g _ _ s

7 _ _ c _ _ - c _ _ _ _ _ _

8 It _ _ _ ia _ _ _ _ _ _ d

9 _ _ _ _ _ z _ _

10 o _ _ _ n _ _ _ _ _

Drinks

11 _ _ _ a

12 b _ _ _ r

13 _ _ _ ff _ _ _

14 _ i _ _ _

15 C _ _ _ _ _ - C _ _ _

Present Simple

I/you/they

2 Write true sentences about <u>you</u>.

1 beer   <u>I like beer. / I don't like beer.</u>

2 swimming _____

3 pizza _____

4 Chinese food _____

5 coffee _____

6 football _____

7 Italian food _____

8 wine _____

9 hamburgers _____

3 Write answers.

4 **T 5.2** Answer the questions. Write true answers about <u>you</u>.

1 Do you speak English? <u>Yes, I do.</u>

2 Do you live in Moscow? <u>No, I don't. I live in Paris.</u>

3 Do you live in England?

_____

4 Do you work in an office?

_____

5 Do you like English?

_____

6 Do you drink coffee?

_____

7 Do you play tennis?

_____

5 Read the text. Answer the questions.

Javier and Jorge

Javier and Jorge are brothers. They're from Chile, but they don't live in Chile now. They live in Spain. They're both doctors and they work in a hospital in Oviedo. They speak Spanish, of course, and they speak English and French.

Javier isn't married but Jorge is. His wife's name is Teresa. They have a house in the country, near Oviedo. Javier's flat is in the centre of Oviedo.

Javier and Jorge like Spanish food and wine. They play sports. They like football and skiing but they don't like tennis or swimming.

1 Do Javier and Jorge live in Chile?
   No, they don't. They live in Spain.

2 Do they work in a hospital?
   Yes, they do.

3 Do they speak Spanish?

   _____

4 Do they speak English and German?

   _____

5 Do Jorge and Teresa live in the centre of Oviedo?

   _____

6 Do Javier and Jorge like Spanish food and wine?

   _____

7 Do they play sports?

   _____

8 Do they like tennis and swimming?

   _____

Questions and answers

6 Put the words in the right order.

1 you / where / do / live / ?
   Where do you live?

2 like / you / Chinese food / do / ?

   _____

3 work / do / where / you / ?

   _____

4 you / drink / do / coffee / ?

   _____

5 like / what sports / you / do / ?

   _____

6 do / speak / how many languages / you / ?

   _____

7 Answer the questions in exercise 6. Write true answers about <u>you</u>.

1 **I live in a** _____

2 _____

3 _____

4 _____

5 _____

6 _____

8 Write questions.

1 Jean-Marie and Hélène work in Paris.
   Do they work in Paris?

2 They have a dog.

   _____

3 They play football.

   _____

4 Pedro and Concha like Coca-Cola.

   _____

5 Olga and Dimitra live near the centre of town.

   _____

6 They drink beer.

   _____

7 They work in a bank.

   _____

9 Complete the sentences with *is*, *are*, or *do*.

1 '**Do** you like skiing?' 'Yes, I _____ .'
2 'Where _____ Jacek from?' 'He _____ from Poland.'
3 '_____ you from France?' 'No, I'm from Germany.'
4 How _____ you spell 'nurse'?
5 Dina and Vicky _____ students.
6 '_____ they live in a flat?' 'Yes, they _____ .'
7 '_____ she a teacher?' 'Yes, she _____ .'
8 What sports _____ they play?

Reading and listening

At a party

10 [T 5.3] Complete the conversation.

Akiko Hello. My (1) **name's** Akiko.
Luc Hi. (2) _____ Luc.
Akiko Where (3) _____ you (4) _____ , Luc?
Luc I'm from France. I (5) _____ in Paris.
Akiko Really? I like Paris.
Luc Where (6) _____ you come (7) _____ ?
Akiko (8) _____ from Japan.
Luc Where in Japan?
Akiko I'm from Tokyo (9) _____ I live
(10) _____ Osaka.
Luc What's (11) _____ job?
Akiko I (12) _____ have a job. I'm (13) _____
student. What's your (14) _____ ?
Luc I (15) _____ in a shop.
Akiko (16) _____ you like it?
Luc It's OK.

Listening

Do you like Bristol?

11 [T 5.4] Listen to the conversation. Who says these things, Paolo or Susan? Write *P* or *S*.

1 I'm from Italy. **P**
2 I live in Bristol. ___
3 I work in a bank. ___
4 Do you like Bristol? ___
5 I live in London. ___
6 I'm a restaurant manager. ___
7 I don't like English food very much. ___

Translation

12 Write the sentences in your language.

1 I like ice-cream.

_____

2 They don't drink coffee.

_____

3 'Do they work in London?' 'No, they don't.'

_____

4 'Do you like your job?' 'Yes, I do.'

_____

Vocabulary and pronunciation

Languages and nationalities

13 **T 5.5** Put the nationalities into the correct columns, A, B, C, or D.

~~German~~ Japanese Brazilian English French Spanish Italian Portuguese

A ●	B ●●	C ●●●	D ●●●●
_____	German	_____	_____
	_____		

14 Write the languages.

2 I'm from England.
I speak _____ .

4 I'm from Italy.
I speak _____

3 I'm from France.
I speak _____ .

1 I'm from Brazil.
I speak **Portuguese** .

5 I'm from Japan.
I speak _____ .

7 I'm from Germany.
I speak _____ .

6 I'm from Spain.
I speak _____ .

15 Write five true sentences.

I	(don't)	drink eat like	Brazilian English French German Italian Portuguese Spanish	beer. cars. coffee. food. houses. wine.

1 **I don't like English food.**

2 _____

3 _____

4 _____

5 _____

6 _____

Everyday English

Numbers and prices

16 **T 5.6** Match the numbers and words.

twenty-three	51
thirty-seven	64
forty-eight	92
fifty-one	37
fifty-five	86
sixty-four	23
seventy-nine	79
eighty-six	48
ninety-two	55

17 Match the prices and words.

17p   two pounds ninety-nine

58p   five p   £26.47

fifteen pounds fifty-five   75p

£99   six pounds forty-nine

one pound sixty-eight   £5.72

5p   ninety-eight p   £6.49

five pounds seventy-two

£2.99   fifty-eight p

three pounds eighty-one   43p

seventy-five p   £3.81

twenty-six pounds forty-seven

seventeen p   98p

£15.55   forty-three p

60p   ninety-nine pounds

£1.68   sixty p

18 **T 5.7** Listen. Write the prices you hear.

1 £3.79

2 _____

3 _____

4 _____

5 _____

6 _____

7 _____

8 _____

19 **T 5.8** Listen to the conversations. Write the prices.

The time • Present Simple – *he/she/it,*
usually/sometimes/never • Questions and negatives – *Yes/No*
questions, *do/does/don't/doesn't* • Days of the week

The time

1 Write the times.

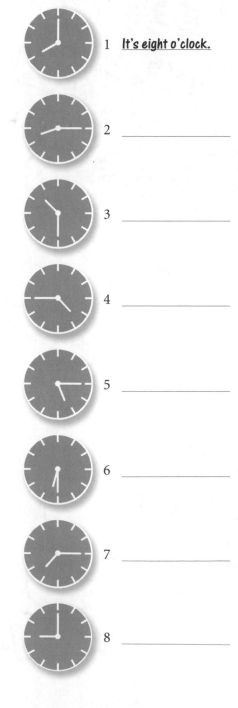

1 *It's eight o'clock.*

2 _____

3 _____

4 _____

5 _____

6 _____

7 _____

8 _____

2 [T 6.1] Listen. Draw the times.

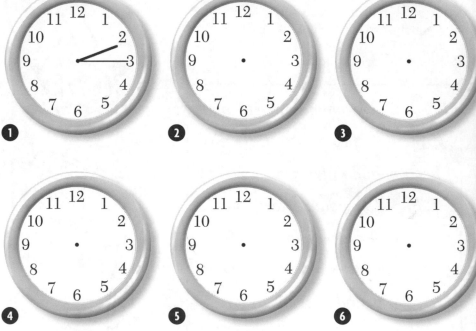

What time do you . . . ?

3 [T 6.2] Answer the questions. Write true answers about <u>you</u>.

1 What time do you get up?

   <u>I get up at</u> _____

2 What time do you have breakfast?

   _____

3 What time do you go to work/school?

   _____

4 What time do you have lunch?

   _____

5 What time do you get home?

   _____

6 What time do you go to bed?

   _____

Present Simple

he/she/it

4 Look at the pictures and complete the sentences about Marta's day.

1 Marta **gets up** at seven thirty.

2 She _____ tea and toast for breakfast.

3 She _____ home at _____ .

4 She _____ to work by car.

5 She _____ a sandwich for lunch.

6 She _____ home at _____ .

7 She sometimes _____ out in the evening.

usually/sometimes/never

5 Write the sentences again with the words in brackets.

1 Marta has breakfast at 7.45. (usually)
   <u>**Marta usually has breakfast at 7.45.**</u>

2 Marta goes to work by bus. (never)
   _____

3 She has a sandwich in her office. (usually)
   _____

4 She leaves work at 5.30. (usually)
   _____

5 She works in the evening. (never)
   _____

6 She goes to a restaurant in the evening. (sometimes)
   _____

6 Write three sentences about you. Use *usually*, *sometimes*, and *never*.

1 <u>**I usually go to work by car.**</u>

2 _____

3 _____

4 _____

Questions and negatives

7 Put the words in the correct order to make questions.

1 Angeles / get up / does / what time / ?

   What time does Angeles get up?

2 live / where / Angeles / does / ?

   _____

3 breakfast / does / have / she / ?

   _____

4 go / when / she / does / to the concert hall / ?

   _____

5 she / usually have / does / lunch / where / ?

   _____

6 she / sometimes do / does / in the afternoon / what / ?

   _____

7 dinner / have / does / she / what time / ?

   _____

8 usually go out / in the evening / she / does / with friends / ?

   _____

Angeles Pérez

Angeles Pérez is a violinist. She plays in the New York Philharmonic. She lives in a flat in Manhattan.

She gets up at six o'clock and has a cup of coffee. She practises the violin until eight o'clock. She doesn't have breakfast. At nine o'clock she goes to the concert hall and plays with the orchestra. She usually has lunch at home. In the afternoon she sometimes goes for a walk in Central Park, and then listens to music.

At six o'clock she cooks dinner and drinks a glass of beer. In the evening she usually goes out with friends. She never listens to music in the evening!

8 **T 6.3** Read and listen to the text. Answer the questions in exercise 7.

1 _She gets up at six o'clock._

2 _____

3 _____

4 _____

5 _____

6 _____

7 _____

8 _____

9 Complete the sentences about Angeles. Use the negative.

1 She **doesn't get** up at seven o'clock.

2 She _____ in a house.

3 She _____ breakfast.

4 She _____ lunch at work.

5 She _____ wine with her dinner.

6 She _____ to music in the evening.

10 Make the sentences negative.

1 Andreas lives in Britain.

   Andreas doesn't live in Britain.

2 Shinji leaves work at one forty-five.

   _____

3 Raoul goes to work by taxi.

   _____

4 Ramiro eats toast for breakfast.

   _____

5 Piet gets home at four thirty.

   _____

6 Oliver speaks French.

   _____

7 Lidia works in a bank.

   _____

8 Raquel has three children.

   _____

Yes/No questions

11 Look at the information about Rosa and Paolo. Write questions and short answers.

	Rosa	Paolo
1 get up early?	✔	✗
2 go to work by car?	✗	✔
3 drink wine?	✔	✗
4 speak English?	✔	✗

Rosa

1 A **Does Rosa get up early?**

  B **Yes, she does.**

2 A _____

  B _____

3 A _____

  B _____

4 A _____

  B _____

Paolo

1 A **Does Paolo get up early?**

  B **No, he doesn't.**

2 A _____

  B _____

3 A _____

  B _____

4 A _____

  B _____

do/does/don't/doesn't

12 Complete the sentences. Use *do*, *does*, *don't*, or *doesn't*.

1 '**Does** he have breakfast?' 'No, he **doesn't** .'

2 We speak Spanish, but we _____ speak French.

3 '_____ you like beer?' 'No, I _____ .'

4 '_____ they usually go out in the evening?' 'Yes, they _____ .'

5 '_____ Françoise live in Spain?' 'Yes, she _____ .'

6 He _____ have an American car. He has a Japanese car.

7 She usually goes to bed at twelve o'clock. She _____ go to bed early.

Translation

13 Write the sentences in your language.

1 She leaves home at eight forty-five.

  _____

2 'Does Idoia live in Manchester?' 'No, she doesn't.'

  _____

3 'Where does Thomas live?' 'In Oxford.'

  _____

4 Maria doesn't go to work by bus.

  _____

5 Osman never stays at home in the evening.

  _____

Vocabulary

14 Complete the crossword.

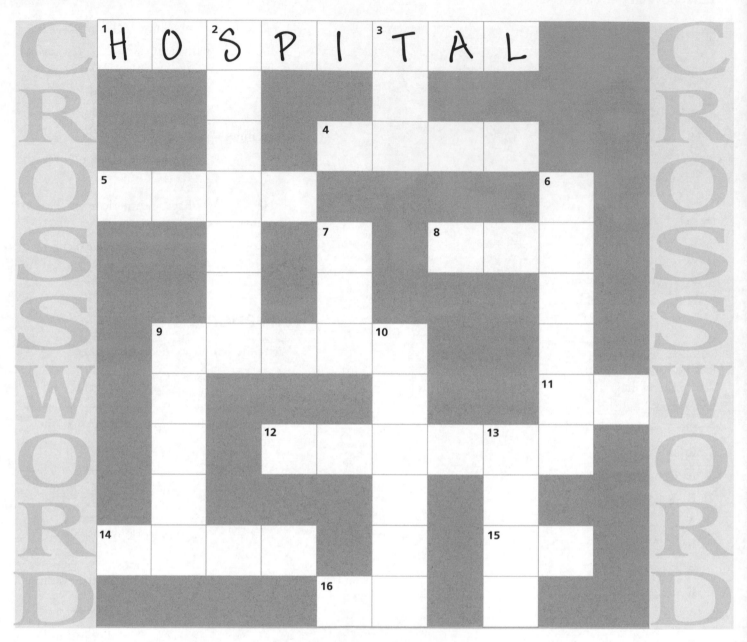

Across ➜

1 Antonella is a doctor. She works in a _____ . (8 letters)

4 Sandra never _____ in restaurants. (4 letters)

5 I usually have a glass of _____ at seven o'clock. (4 letters)

8 She has a German _____ . It's a BMW. (3 letters)

9 'What's your _____ number?' '243806.' (5 letters)

11 'Are you from Canada?' 'Yes, I _____ .' (2 letters)

12 ten, _____ , thirty, forty, fifty … (6 letters)

14 'What's your job?' 'I'm a _____ driver.' (4 letters)

15 'What's your name?' '_____ name's Joseph.' (2 letters)

16 She's _____ artist. (2 letters)

Down ↓

2 He lives in Spain, but he doesn't speak _____ . (7 letters)

3 Do you want _____ or coffee? (3 letters)

6 Today is Thursday. Tomorrow is _____ . (6 letters)

7 We have two children – a daughter and a _____ . (3 letters)

9 'Do you like _____ ?' 'No, I don't like Italian food.' (5 letters)

10 6 + 5 = _____ (6 letters)

13 'What _____ is it, please?' 'It's ten o'clock.' (4 letters)

Listening

Anna's day

15 **T 6.4** Listen. What does Anna do at these times?

1 10.00 in the evening
   She goes to work.

2 6.15 in the morning
   _____

3 7.30 in the morning
   _____

4 3.00 in the afternoon
   _____

5 3.30 in the afternoon
   _____

6 8.30 in the evening
   _____

Writing

Your day

16 Write about your day. Use the words in the box.

> play   have breakfast/lunch/dinner   go to school/work
> get home   get up   listen to music   watch television
> go shopping   in the morning/afternoon/evening
> usually/sometimes/never   stay at home   go out

_____
_____
_____
_____
_____
_____
_____
_____
_____
_____

Everyday English

Days of the week

17 Write the days of the week.

1 o d m y n a   = _Monday_
2 r y f a d i   = _____
3 d y e t a s u   = _____
4 t y u s h d r a = _____
5 d u s a y n   = _____
6 d w y s e e a d n = _____
7 a d t y r s u a = _____

18 Write the days of the week in the correct order.

Sunday

_____
_____
_____
_____
_____
_____

in/on/at

19 Complete the sentences. Use *in*, *on*, or *at*.

1 I play tennis **on** Saturday morning.

2 I usually have lunch _____ one o'clock.

3 I never get up late _____ Sunday morning.

4 What do you do _____ the weekend?

5 We sometimes listen to the radio _____ the evening.

6 _____ Wednesday I sometimes go swimming.

7 _____ the morning he works at home.

8 'What time do you leave work?' '_____ five thirty.'

9 They usually stay at home _____ the afternoon.

Object pronouns • *this/that* • Question words
why and *because* • Adjectives • *Can I...?*

Object pronouns

1 Complete the chart.

Subject pronouns	Object pronouns
I	me
you	___
he	___
she	___
it	___
we	___
they	___

2 Choose the correct words.

1 Do you like (him) / he?
2 This is a photo of *she* / *her*.
3 He likes *their* / *them* very much.
4 You never listen to *me* / *my*!
5 Mr Jones teaches *us* / *we* English.
6 She likes *you* / *your* very much.

3 Complete the sentences. Use object pronouns.

1 I don't watch TV in the afternoon. I watch **it** in the evening.
2 'Do you like hamburgers?' 'No, I hate _____ !'
3 'Do you love Pete?' 'No, but I like _____ very much.'
4 I don't have lunch at home. I have _____ at the office.
5 My grandparents live near our house. They always visit _____ at the weekend.
6 'Is that a photo of _____ ?' 'Yes, it is. I'm with my husband, David.'

this/that

4 **T 7.1** Write questions and answers.

 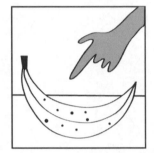 

1 A **What's that?**
  B **It's a hat.**

2 A **What's this?**
  B **It's a banana.**

3 A _____
  B _____

4 A _____
  B _____

5 A _____
  B _____

6 A _____
  B _____

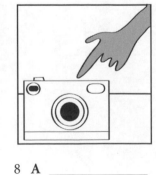 

7 A _____
  B _____

8 A _____
  B _____

9 A _____
  B _____

5 Write sentences.

1 **This is a phone.**

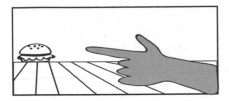

2 **That's a hamburger.**

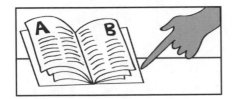

3 _____

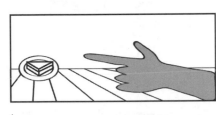

4 _____

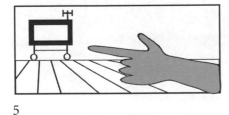

5 _____

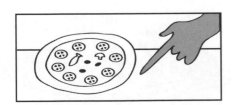

6 _____

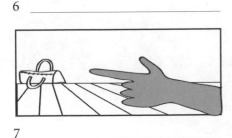

7 _____

Question words

6 Match a question word in A with an answer in B.

A	B
1 What … ?	a By car.
2 How … ?	b Two. Tennis and football.
3 Where … ?	c Céline Dion.
4 Who … ?	d £14.99.
5 Why … ?	e A sandwich and a Coke.
6 How old … ?	f I'm 28.
7 What time … ?	g At nine o'clock in the morning.
8 How much … ?	h In Madrid.
9 How many … ?	i Because she doesn't have a car.

7 Write questions. Then choose an answer from B in exercise 6.

1 does / for lunch / have / what / Emily / ?
  What does Emily have for lunch?   Answer: _e_

2 that / how much / dictionary / is / ?
  _____   Answer: ___

3 you / do / what time / start work / ?
  _____   Answer: ___

4 Pierre / to work / how / does / go / ?
  _____   Answer: ___

5 play / do / how many / you / sports / ?
  _____   Answer: ___

6 to school / walk / Sandra / does / why / ?
  _____   Answer: ___

7 does / live / where / Maria / ?
  _____   Answer: ___

8 favourite pop star / your / who / is / ?
  _____   Answer: ___

9 old / how / you / are / ?
  _____   Answer: ___

8 **T 7.2** Answer the questions. Write true answers about <u>you</u>.

1 Where do you usually go on holiday?
  _____

2 What music do you listen to?
  _____

3 Who do you like on TV?
  _____

4 Why do you want to learn English?
  _____

5 How many brothers and sisters do you have?
  _____

why and *because*

9 Match the questions and answers.

Questions

1 Why do you go to the beach every day? *d*

2 Why don't you drink beer? ___

3 Why do you always have pizza for lunch? ___

4 Why do you get up at ten o'clock? ___

5 Why do you live in the country? ___

Answers

a Because I don't like the city!

b Because I don't start work until eleven o'clock.

c Because I like Italian food.

d Because I love swimming.

e Because I don't like it.

Listening

An interview with Dan Brat

10 **T 7.3** Listen to the interview with Dan Brat. Choose the correct answers.

1 Dan has *four* / *five* houses.

2 Dan's favourite house is in *Hollywood* / *Hawaii*.

3 Dan *is* / *isn't* married.

4 Billy-Jo is *wife number five* / *wife number nine*.

5 Dan and Billy-Jo *always* / *never* work together.

6 Dan *likes* / *doesn't like* her movies.

7 Dan has *six* / *seven* / *eight* children.

Vocabulary

Adjectives

11 **T 7.4** Match the words and pictures.

| big | cheap | ~~cold~~ | expensive | horrible |
| hot | lovely | new | old | small |

1 *cold*   6 _____

2 _____   7 _____

3 _____   8 _____

4 _____   9 _____

5 _____   10 _____

Pablo   Pilar

Alberto

Sarah

5 Alain

6 Judit

7 £2000 Maurice

8 Yumi £200

9 Keith

10 Catherine

12 Write sentences about the pictures in exercise 11.

1 _Pablo's coffee is cold._

2 _____

3 _____

4 _____

5 _____

6 _____

7 _____

8 _____

9 _____

10 _____

13 Write one word in each sentence. Choose *a* or *an* where necessary.

> big ~~expensive~~ friendly horrible
> lovely new old small cheap

1 I like **expensive** cars.

2 I have *a / an* _____ computer.

3 I live in *a / an* _____ house/flat.

4 I have *a / an* _____ dictionary.

5 I have *a / an* _____ TV.

6 I am _____ !

Translation

14 Write the sentences in your language.

1 How much money do you have?

_____

2 'Why don't you like him?' 'Because he's horrible!'

_____

3 'What's that?' 'It's a computer.'

_____

4 This is a camera.

_____

5 It's a beautiful old building.

_____

Reading

A postcard from San Francisco

15 Read the postcard.
Correct the sentences.

Dear Eva,
I'm in San Francisco. I'm on holiday with my friend Mark. San Francisco is a beautiful city, but the buildings aren't very old. The people are very friendly and the food is fantastic (and very cheap!). Our hotel is near the centre of the city. It's very modern and cheap, but it isn't very comfortable.
The weather is very hot. We go to the beach every day. I love swimming in the Pacific Ocean!
See you soon.
Love,
Tom

Eva Ejsmond

43 Smith Street

London SW3 4EP

England

San Francisco

1 Tom is in San Diego.
Tom is in San Francisco.

2 The buildings in San Francisco are very old.

3 The food is horrible.

4 The food is expensive.

5 The hotel is very old.

6 The hotel is cheap and comfortable.

7 The weather is cold.

8 They go shopping every day.

Everyday English

Can I ...?

16 **T 7.5** Listen. Match the conversations and photos.

Conversation	1	2	3	4	5
Picture	e				

17 **T 7.5** Put the sentences in the correct place in the conversations.

> Can I have a pizza, please?
> How much is it?
> How much is it?
> ~~Can I try on this jacket, please?~~
> £2.30.
> Can I have a ticket to London, please?
> Can I send an email, please?
> Here's your ticket and £5 change.
> Can I help you?

1 **A** <u>Can I try on this jacket, please?</u>

   B Of course. The changing rooms are just here.

2 **A** _____

   B Sure. Single or return?

   A Single, please.

   B That's £15, please.

   A There you are.

   B Thank you. £20. _____

   _____

3 **A** _____

   B OK. PC Number 15.

   A _____

   B 1p a minute. Pay at the end, please.

4 **A** Good afternoon. _____

   B Yes, can I change this traveller's cheque, please?

   A Of course. _____

   B £50.

5 **A** _____

   B There you are.

   A How much is it?

   B _____

   A Thank you.

   B £5. Here's £2.70 change.

Rooms and furniture • *There is/are*
Prepositions • Directions

Where I live

Rooms and furniture

1 **T 8.1** What are the rooms?

1 i v i l g n   m o r o
   living room

2 t h r a m b o o
   _____

3 l o i t t e
   _____

4 i g n d i n   o m o r
   _____

5 k e n c h i t
   _____

6 d r e o b o m
   _____

2 Look at the picture. Write the names of the rooms.

A *bedroom*   _____

B _____

C _____

D _____

E _____

F _____

3 **T 8.2** Match the words to the numbers in the picture in exercise 2.

| armchair ~~bed~~ CD player cooker lamp magazine picture shower sofa table TV video recorder |

1 _bed_   7 _____
2 _____ 8 _____
3 _____ 9 _____
4 _____ 10 _____
5 _____ 11 _____
6 _____ 12 _____

There is/are

4 Look at the picture. Make six sentences with *There is / There's* ... and *There are* ... .

1 _There are two armchairs in the living room._
2 _There's a cat in the kitchen._
3 _____
4 _____
5 _____
6 _____
7 _____
8 _____

5 **T 8.3** Look at the picture. Then write short answers.

1 Is there a TV in the dining room? _No, there isn't._
2 Are there any books in the living room? _Yes, there are._
3 Is there a table in the kitchen?

_____

4 Are there any chairs in the bathroom?

_____

5 Is there a sofa in the living room?

_____

6 Are there any books in the dining room?

_____

7 Is there a magazine in the toilet?

_____

8 Are there any armchairs in the living room?

_____

6 **T 8.4** Look at the picture. Then write questions and answers.

1 TV / bedroom / ?

  A _Is there a TV in the bedroom ?_

  B _Yes, there is._

2 chairs / kitchen / ?

  A _Are there any chairs in the kitchen?_

  B _No, there aren't._

3 magazine /living room / ?

  A _____

  B _____

4 pictures / dining room / ?

  A _____

  B _____

5 picture / toilet / ?

  A _____

  B _____

6 TV / bathroom / ?

  A _____

  B _____

7 CDs / bedroom / ?

  A _____

  B _____

8 table / dining room / ?

  A _____

  B _____

7 Match a question in A with an answer in B.

A	B
1 Is Manolo in the living room?	a Yes, there are.
2 Is there a table in the bathroom?	b No, he isn't.
3 Is this your book?	c Yes, they are.
4 Is Corrine from Britain?	d No, there isn't.
5 Are there any magazines on the table?	e Yes, it is.
6 Are Kim and Frances married?	f No, she isn't.

8 **T 8.5** **Answer the questions. Write true answers about you.**

1 How many rooms are there in your house or flat? _____

2 Is there a CD player? _____

3 Is there a TV in your bedroom? _____

4 Is there a shower in the bathroom? _____

5 Are there any books or magazines in the toilet? _____

Pronunciation

9 **T 8.6** Where is the stress? Put the words into the correct columns.

afternoon armchair because computer
delicious dictionary expensive fantastic
holiday horrible Japan ~~kitchen~~ languages
lovely magazine never Portuguese until

A	B	C	D	E
●●	●●	●●●	●●●	●●●
kitchen				

Prepositions

10 Label the pictures. Use *in*, *on*, *under*, and *next to*.

1 **under**

2 _____

3 _____

4 _____

11 Complete the sentences. Use *in*, *on*, *under*, or *next to*.

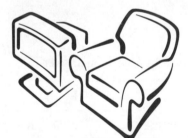

1 The TV is **next to** the armchair.

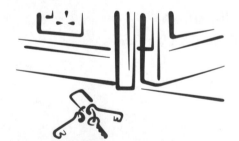

2 The keys are _____ the floor.

3 The mobile phone is _____ the drawer.

4 The magazine is _____ the sofa.

5 The camera is _____ the table _____ the lamp.

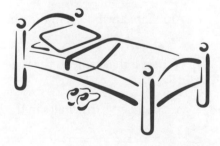

6 The shoes are _____ the floor _____ the bed.

12 **T 8.7** Listen and draw the things in the room.

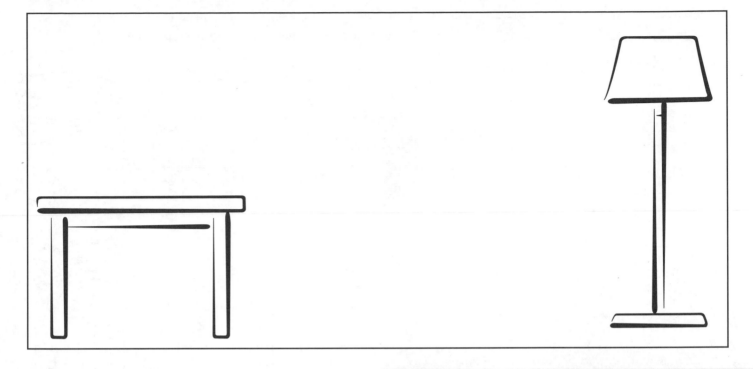

Reading and writing

Our house

13 **T 8.8** Read and listen to the text. Answer the questions. Write sentences.

1 Where do Lucy and Nicolas live?

   <u>They live in a small, old house in Brighton.</u>

2 How many bedrooms are there in their house?

   _____

3 Is there a sofa in the living room?

   _____

4 What do Lucy and Nicolas do in the evening?

   _____

5 Where are there photographs of their families?

   _____

6 Is the kitchen old?

   _____

7 Where do Lucy and Nicolas have lunch?

   _____

8 Is there a garden?

   _____

9 Are Lucy and Nicolas happy in their house?

   _____

Lucy and Nicolas

We live in a small, old house in Brighton. It has two bedrooms, a living room, a dining room, a kitchen – and there's a bathroom, of course!

In the living room there are two armchairs and a sofa. We also have a television, a video recorder, and a CD player. On the wall there are two pictures. It's a very comfortable room, and in the evening we sit and watch television or listen to music.

In the dining room there is a table and four chairs. There are a lot of photographs of our families on the walls. The kitchen is new. We have breakfast in the kitchen, but we have lunch and dinner in the dining room.

We have a small garden and two cats. We are very happy in our house!

14 Write about your house or flat.

_____
_____
_____
_____
_____
_____
_____
_____
_____
_____

Translation

15 Write the sentences in your language.

1   There's a table in the dining room.

_____
_____

2   There are three armchairs in the living room.

_____
_____

3   'Is there a picture on the wall?'
    'Yes, there is.'

_____
_____

4   'Are there any magazines under the bed?'
    'No, there aren't.'

_____
_____

Everyday English

Directions

16 Find the places. They are all on the map on p49.

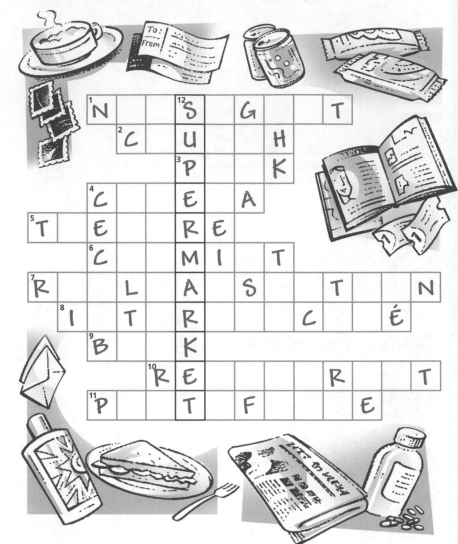

17 [T 8.9] Listen and look at the map on p49. Follow the directions. Where are you?

1   Start from the **Chinese restaurant**.

You are at the _theatre_.

2   Start from the **theatre**.

You are at the _____ .

3   Start from the **chemist**.

You are at the _____ .

4   Start from the **railway station**.

You are at the _____ .

5   Start from the **Internet café**.

You are at the _____ .

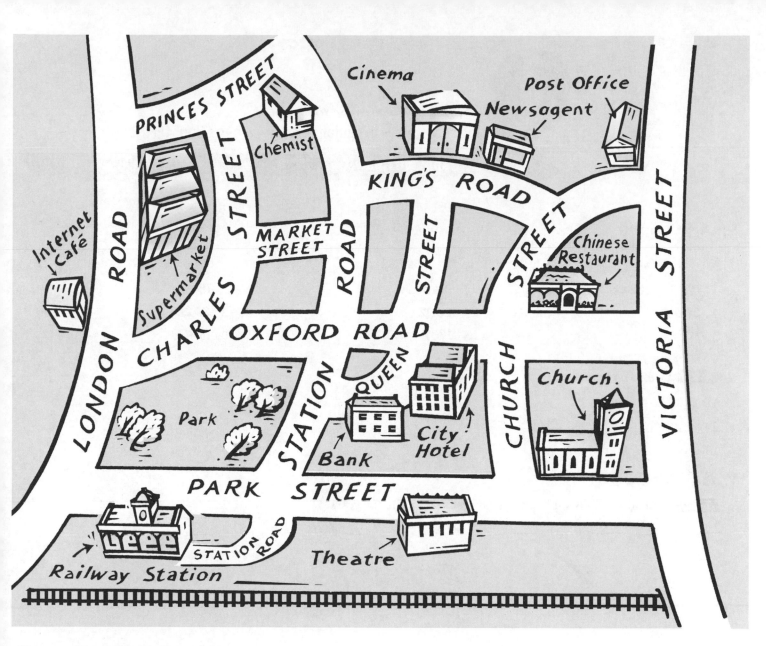

18 Complete the conversations. Write directions.

1 Start from the chemist.

   A Excuse me. Is there a bank near here?

   B <u>Yes, go down Station Road. Go past King's Road</u>
   <u>and Oxford Road. Turn left into Queen Street.</u>
   <u>The bank is on the right.</u>

2 Start from the theatre.

   A Excuse me. Is there a supermarket near here?

   B _____

   _____

   _____

   _____

3 Start from the post office.

   A Excuse me. Is there a bank near here?

   B _____

   _____

   _____

   _____

   _____

4 Start from the railway station.

   A Excuse me. Is there a cinema near here?

   B _____

   _____

   _____

   _____

Saying years • *was/were born*
Past Simple – irregular verbs • When's your birthday?

Happy birthday!

Saying years

1 Write the years.

1 *1980* nineteen eighty   4 *1848* _____   7 *1815* _____

2 *2000* _____   5 *2002* _____   8 *2020* _____

3 *1999* _____   6 *1987* _____   9 *1945* _____

2 [T 9.1] Listen. Write the years.

1 <u>2005</u>   3 _____   5 _____   7 _____

2 _____   4 _____   6 _____   8 _____

was/were born

3 [T 9.2] Look at the family. Listen to Francesca and write the years.

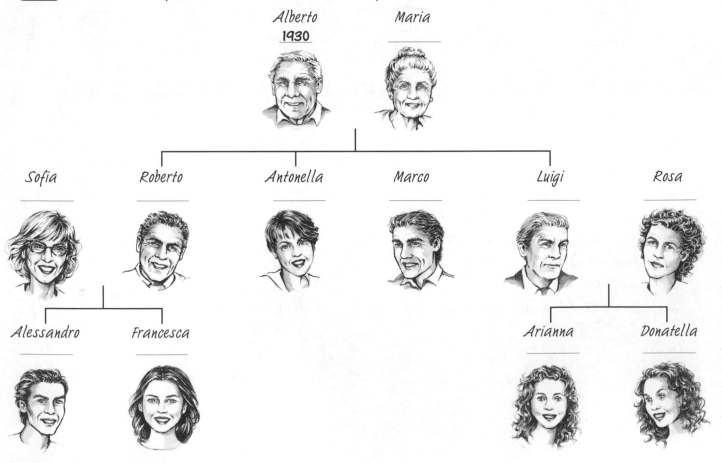

4 Write questions and answers.

1 Maria

  A <u>When was Maria born?</u>

  B <u>She was born in 1930.</u>

2 Alessandro

  A _____

  B _____

3 Arianna and Donatella

  A _____

  B _____

4 Antonella and Rosa

  A _____

  B _____

5 Roberto

  A _____

  B _____

6 Marco

  A _____

  B _____

7 Sofia and Luigi

  A _____

  B _____

8 Francesca

  A _____

  B _____

9 Alberto and Maria

  A _____

  B _____

5 Write five sentences about people in your family.

1 <u>My mother was born in</u> _____

2 _____

  _____

3 _____

  _____

4 _____

  _____

5 _____

  _____

Writing

Famous people

6 Look at the information about William Shakespeare and complete the text.

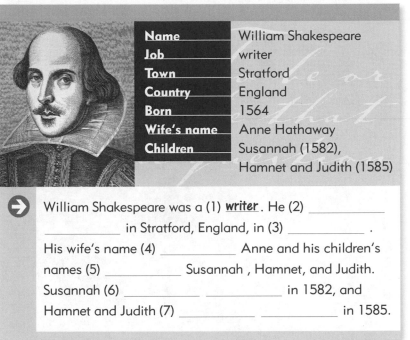

Name	William Shakespeare
Job	writer
Town	Stratford
Country	England
Born	1564
Wife's name	Anne Hathaway
Children	Susannah (1582), Hamnet and Judith (1585)

→ William Shakespeare was a (1) <u>writer</u>. He (2) _____ _____ in Stratford, England, in (3) _____ .
His wife's name (4) _____ Anne and his children's names (5) _____ Susannah , Hamnet, and Judith.
Susannah (6) _____ _____ in 1582, and Hamnet and Judith (7) _____ _____ in 1585.

7 Look at the information about Mozart and write a text.

Name	Wolfgang Amadeus Mozart
Job	musician
Town	Salzburg
Country	Austria
Born	1756
Wife's name	Constanze
Children	Carl (1784) Franz (1791)

→ _____

_____

_____

_____

_____

_____

_____

_____

_____

8 Write questions and answers about Amy Johnson.

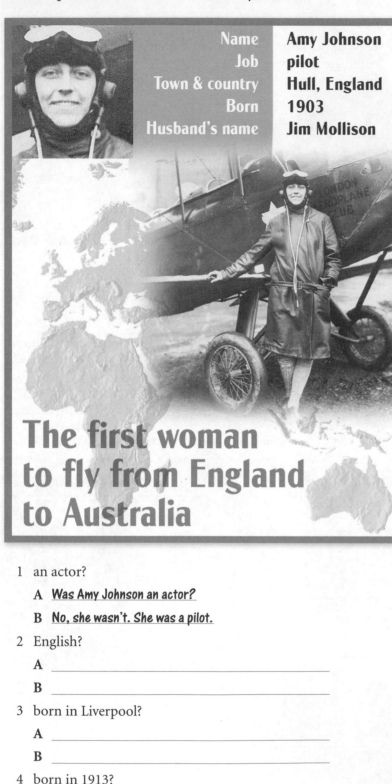

Name	Amy Johnson
Job	pilot
Town & country	Hull, England
Born	1903
Husband's name	Jim Mollison

The first woman to fly from England to Australia

1 an actor?

  A <u>Was Amy Johnson an actor?</u>

  B <u>No, she wasn't. She was a pilot.</u>

2 English?

  A _____

  B _____

3 born in Liverpool?

  A _____

  B _____

4 born in 1913?

  A _____

  B _____

5 husband's name Jim Mollison?

  A _____

  B _____

9 Write negative and positive sentences.

1 Mozart: German ✘ Austrian ✔

  <u>Mozart wasn't German.</u>
  <u>He was Austrian.</u>

2 Charles Dickens: musician ✘ writer ✔

  _____

  _____

3 Agatha Christie: from Scotland ✘ from England ✔

  _____

  _____

4 Bill Clinton: President of Canada ✘ President of the USA ✔

  _____

  _____

5 Marie Curie: French ✘ Polish ✔

  _____

  _____

6 Laurel and Hardy: Australian ✘ American ✔

  _____

  _____

7 Humphrey Bogart and Ingrid Bergman: singers ✘ actors ✔

  _____

  _____

10 Complete the sentences. Use *was*, *were*, *wasn't*, and *weren't*.

1 I <u>**was**</u> in London yesterday.

2 '_____ she at home yesterday afternoon?' 'No, she _____.'

3 They _____ born in Italy. They _____ born in Spain. They're Spanish.

4 'Where _____ you born?' 'I _____ born in France.'

5 '_____ you at the office yesterday?' 'No, we _____.'

6 '_____ he born in 1985?' 'No, he _____ born in 1985. He _____ born in 1975.'

Past Simple – irregular verbs

11 **T 9.3** Complete the irregular forms. Use *a, e, i, o,* and *u.*

1 am/is	w **a** s	5 say	s _ _ d
2 are	w _ r _	6 see	s _ w
3 buy	b _ _ g h t	7 take	t _ _ k
4 go	w _ n t		

12 Complete the text. Use the irregular verbs in the box.

> bought   said   saw   saw   took
> was   ~~went~~   went   were

1 My name's Sam Smith. I'm a writer and I work at home. There's a computer in my office, but it's very old.

2 So, yesterday morning I (1) **went** to London to buy a new computer.

3 I (2) _____ a lot of computers in shops in Oxford Street, but they (3) _____ very expensive.

4 ...en I (4) _____ to ...small shop near Hyde ...rk. The computers ...ere were very cheap.

5 I (5) _____ a computer for £499. The shop assistant (6) _____ : 'It's very good and it's very cheap.'

6 I (7) _____ the computer home.

7 But yesterday evening I (8) _____ the same computer on television. It (9) _____ £299! I was very upset!

Translation

13 Write the sentences in your language.

1 When were you born?

_____

2 Michelangelo was a painter.

_____

3 They weren't at home yesterday.

_____

4 I went shopping yesterday afternoon.

_____

5 I bought a new CD player.

_____

Vocabulary

14 **T 9.4** Write the words in the correct columns.

armchair   daughter   watch   big   wine   bed
bank   dining room   horrible   husband   ~~ice-cream~~
kitchen   table   listen   nurse   old   parents   play
post office   railway station   Sunday   tea   teacher
Thursday   bathroom   Wednesday   businessman

Food & drink	Jobs	Rooms
ice-cream		
Places	**Family**	**Days of the week**
Furniture	**Verbs**	**Adjectives**

Everyday English

When's your birthday?

15 Write the months.

1	r a y u j a n	January
2	l u j y	_____
3	l a i p r	_____
4	d e m e b e r c	_____
5	r c o b o e t	_____
6	y b r f r e a u	_____
7	b e m e p e s t r	_____
8	n u e j	_____
9	t u u a s g	_____
10	a h m c r	_____
11	e r b n e o m v	_____
12	y a m	_____

16 Write the months in the correct order.

January

_____

_____

_____

_____

_____

_____

_____

_____

17 **T 9.5** Match the numbers and words.

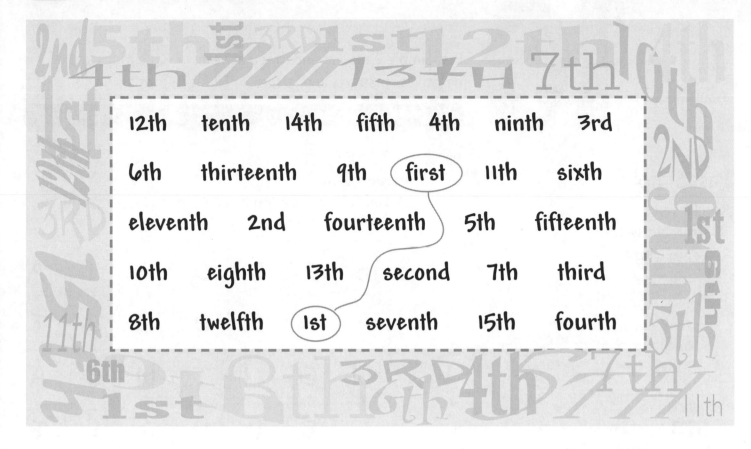

12th	tenth	14th	fifth	4th	ninth	3rd
6th	thirteenth	9th	first	11th	sixth
eleventh	2nd	fourteenth	5th	fifteenth
10th	eighth	13th	second	7th	third
8th	twelfth	1st	seventh	15th	fourth

18 **T 9.6** Listen. Write the dates.

1 <u>January 3rd</u>
2 _____
3 _____
4 _____
5 _____
6 _____
7 _____
8 _____
9 _____
10 _____
11 _____
12 _____
13 _____

19 Write six true sentences about your family and your friends' birthdays.

1 <u>My mother's birthday is on June 5th.</u>
2 _____
3 _____
4 _____
5 _____
6 _____
7 _____

Past Simple – regular and irregular verbs • Questions and negatives • Sports and leisure • Filling in forms

We had a good time!

Past Simple

Regular verbs

1 Write the past tense forms.

1 play **played**

2 cook _____

3 stay _____

4 work _____

5 listen _____

6 watch _____

Pronunciation

2 **T 10.1** Put the verbs from exercise 1 into the correct columns, A or B.

A	B
/t/	/d/
_____	**played**
_____	_____
_____	_____

3 Complete the sentences. Use the verbs from exercise 1.

1 Kate and David **stayed** at home yesterday evening.

2 I _____ to the radio yesterday afternoon.

3 We _____ television from five o'clock until nine o'clock.

4 Madeleine _____ a delicious meal for us yesterday evening.

5 Pam _____ at her computer yesterday morning.

6 Ben _____ football on Saturday.

Irregular verbs

4 Find the past tense forms of these verbs: *buy, eat, get up, go, have, see.*

S	A	D	G	D	T	A
A	N	F	O	U	G	T
W	E	N	T	N	E	A
E	B	O	U	G	H	T
N	F	W	P	U	A	E
K	A	T	P	S	D	M

5 Complete the text. Use the verbs from exercise 4.

Naomi (1) **got up** at eight o'clock yesterday morning and (2) _____ a shower. At ten o'clock she (3) _____ for a walk. She (4) _____ a magazine and a sandwich at the newsagent. The weather was lovely, so she (5) _____ the sandwich in the park. In the afternoon she (6) _____ her friends, Cathy and Vicky.

Listening

Mike's day

6 **T 10.2** Listen to Mike. Put the pictures in the correct order.

a ☐　　b ☐　　c 1

d ☐　　e ☐　　f ☐

g ☐　　h ☐　　i ☐

7 **T 10.2** Listen again. Are the sentences true (✔) or false (✘)?

1　Yesterday Mike got up at eleven o'clock.　☒　　　4　He liked the film.　☐

2　He went to work at eight-thirty.　☐　　　5　Mike stayed at home in the evening.　☐

3　He had lunch with his family.　☐　　　6　He had a shower at nine o'clock.　☐

Writing

Last Saturday

8 Write about what you did last Saturday.

_____
_____
_____
_____
_____
_____
_____
_____
_____

Questions and negatives

9 **T 10.3** Write questions and answers about Emilio.

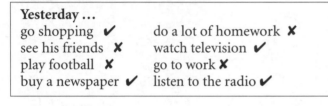

Yesterday …

go shopping ✔	do a lot of homework ✘
see his friends ✘	watch television ✔
play football ✘	go to work ✘
buy a newspaper ✔	listen to the radio ✔

1 **A** <u>*Did Emilio go shopping yesterday?*</u>

  B <u>*Yes, he did.*</u>

2 **A** <u>*Did he see his friends ?*</u>

  B <u>*No, he didn't.*</u>

3 **A** _____

  B _____

4 **A** _____

  B _____

5 **A** _____

  B _____

6 **A** _____

  B _____

7 **A** _____

  B _____

8 **A** _____

  B _____

10 Write questions.

1 do / you / yesterday morning / did / what / ?

What did you do yesterday morning?

2 last weekend / who / you / did / see / ?

_____

3 did / get home / what time / yesterday evening / you / ?

_____

4 homework / you / last week / did / how much / do / ?

_____

5 this morning / what / you / have / did / for breakfast / ?

_____

6 where / you / did / yesterday / lunch / have / ?

_____

_____

11 Answer the questions in exercise 10. Write about <u>you</u>.

1 _____

_____

2 _____

_____

3 _____

_____

4 _____

_____

5 _____

_____

6 _____

12 Write negative sentences.

1 She went to a party yesterday evening.

She didn't go to a party yesterday evening.

2 We saw our friends yesterday.

_____

3 They got up late yesterday morning.

_____

4 You played tennis.

_____

5 I had a big breakfast.

_____

6 He did a lot of housework at the weekend.

_____

7 We watched a film on TV yesterday evening.

_____

8 Last week I stayed in a hotel in Paris.

_____

Translation

13 Write the sentences in your language.

1 She watched television yesterday evening.

_____

2 I went to London yesterday.

_____

3 They didn't see their friends.

_____

4 'Did you get up late?' 'Yes, I did.'

_____

5 What did you do yesterday morning?

_____

Vocabulary

Sports and leisure

14 **T 10.4** Match the words and pictures. Then write *go* or *play*.

> baseball   cards   dancing   football   golf
> ice-hockey   ice-skating   sailing   skiing
> ~~tennis~~   walking   windsurfing

1 **play** **tennis**
2 _____   _____
3 _____   _____
4 _____   _____
5 _____   _____
6 _____   _____
7 _____   _____
8 _____   _____
9 _____   _____
10 _____   _____
11 _____   _____
12 _____   _____

Reading

Ned's holiday

15 Read the text. Correct the sentences.

1 Last summer Ned and Hannah went to Spain.
   They didn't go to Spain. They went to Italy.

2 They had a terrible time.
   _____
   _____

3 They stayed in a hotel.
   _____
   _____

4 Every morning they got up at eleven o'clock.
   _____
   _____

Last summer my wife, Hannah, and I went on holiday to Italy. We had a really good time. We stayed in a house with our friends, Graham and Rachel.

Every morning we got up at nine o'clock and cooked breakfast. Then we went swimming. The weather was lovely – hot and sunny. We usually had lunch in a café near the beach. Hannah and Rachel usually played tennis in the afternoon, but Graham and I went windsurfing or played golf.

In the evening we cooked a big meal in the house and then went dancing. We got home very late and then usually played cards. We never went to bed early!

5 The weather was horrible.

_____

_____

6 Hannah and Rachel played golf in the afternoon.

_____

_____

7 In the evening they had a meal in a restaurant.

_____

_____

8 After dinner they went swimming.

_____

_____

Everyday English

Filling in forms

16 **T 10.5** Listen to the conversation in the sports centre. Fill in the form.

arena
Sports Centre

APPLICATION FORM

Mr ☐ Mrs ☐ Miss ☐ Ms ☐ (please tick)

Full name ....

Address ....

....

....

Postcode ....

Phone number ....

Date of birth ....

Nationality ....

What sports are you interested in? (please circle)

| swimming | squash | fitness training |
| basketball | athletics | tennis |

11

Activities • *can/can't* • Requests and offers
What's the problem?

We can do it!

Activities

1 **T 11.1** Match the words and pictures.

| drive a car   ~~make a cake~~   play the guitar |
| play the piano   run   speak French |
| use a computer   draw   ride a horse |

1 <u>make a cake</u>
2 _____
3 _____
4 _____
5 _____
6 _____
7 _____
8 _____
9 _____

*Bonjour.
Ça va?*

can/can't

2 Write about you. Write three sentences with *can* and three sentences with *can't*. Use the activities in exercise 1.

1 _I can draw._

2 _I can't make a cake._

3 _____

4 _____

5 _____

6 _____

7 _____

8 _____

3 **T 11.2** Write sentences.

	Bill	**Amanda**	**Jill and Sam**
read music	✔	✗	✔
use a computer	✔	✗	✔
ride a horse	✗	✔	✗

1 Bill / read music

   Bill can read music.

2 Amanda / use a computer

   Amanda can't use a computer.

3 Bill / use a computer

   _____

4 Bill / ride a horse

   _____

5 Amanda / read music

   _____

6 Amanda / ride a horse

   _____

7 Jill and Sam / read music

   _____

8 Jill and Sam / use a computer

   _____

9 Jill and Sam / ride a horse

   _____

4 **T 11.3** Write questions and answers.

1 Amanda / read music?

   A _Can Amanda read music?_   B _No, she can't._

2 Bill / use a computer?

   A _Can Bill use a computer?_   B _Yes, he can._

3 Bill / read music?

   A _____

   B _____

4 Bill / ride a horse?

   A _____

   B _____

5 Amanda / use a computer?

   A _____

   B _____

6 Amanda / ride a horse?

   A _____

   B _____

7 Jill and Sam / read music?

   A _____

   B _____

8 Jill and Sam / use a computer?

   A _____

   B _____

9 Jill and Sam / ride a horse?

   A _____

   B _____

5 **T 11.4** Answer the questions about you.

1 Can you drive?

   _____

2 Can you read music?

   _____

3 Can you swim?

   _____

4 Can you ski?

   _____

5 Can you cook?

   _____

6 Can you understand Japanese?

   _____

Listening

Can I be in your pop group?

6 **T 11.5** Lisa wants to be in the pop group, *Raincloud*. Listen to the interview and choose the correct answers.

1 Lisa (*has*) / *doesn't have* all *Raincloud*'s CDs.

2 Lisa *can* / *can't* play the guitar.

3 Lisa *can* / *can't* play the piano.

4 Lisa *can* / *can't* read music very well.

5 Last year *Raincloud* were on tour in *France* / *Ireland*.

6 Lisa *can* / *can't* drive.

7 Lisa *can* / *can't* speak French.

8 Lisa *can* / *can't* understand German.

9 Lisa *can* / *can't* speak German very well.

Pronunciation

7 **T 11.6** Listen and repeat.

/kən/	/kæn/	/kɑːnt/
Can you swim?	● Yes, I can.	● I can't swim.

8 **T 11.7** Listen to the sentences. Tick the pronunciation of *can/can't* in each sentence.

	A	B	C
	can /kən/	● **can** /kæn/	● **can't** /kɑːnt/
1	✔		
2			
3			
4			
5			
6			
7			

Requests and offers

9 Write one question with *Can …* in each picture. Use the words in the box.

> ~~come to my party~~   have a pizza, please   help you
> speak more slowly, please   tell me the time, please

❶
Can you come to my party?

When is it?

❷
_____ ?

_____

❸
_____ ?

_____

④

⑤

Translation

11 Write the sentences in your language.

1 I can play the piano.

_____

2 Ben can't speak French.

_____

3 'Can you cook?' 'Yes, I can.'

_____

4 Can you speak more slowly, please?

_____

5 Can I have a coffee, please?

_____

6 Can I help you?

_____

Vocabulary

Odd one out

12 Which word is different?

1 mother	father	(teacher)	brother
2 December	autumn	summer	spring
3 swimming	windsurfing	football	sailing
4 March	September	Tuesday	May
5 weekend	morning	afternoon	evening
6 listened	bought	cooked	stayed
7 living room	dining room	kitchen	garden

10 Now write the answers to the questions in exercise 9.

I'm sorry. Can you understand now?
It's about ten forty-five.
~~When is it?~~
Yes, I want to buy this newspaper.
Yes, of course. Small, medium, or large?

Everyday English

What's the problem?

13 Match the conversations and the pictures.

A I forgot your birthday. I'm really sorry.
A This computer doesn't work.

B It doesn't matter.
B Check it in your dictionary.

A What's the matter?
A I can't find my plane ticket.

B Did you push this button?
B The CD player's broken.

A I'm lost. Can you help me?
A I don't understand this word.

B Where do you want to go?
B You put it on the table.

1 **A** I forgot your birthday. I'm really sorry.
  B It doesn't matter.

2 **A** _____
  B _____

3 **A** _____
  B _____

4 **A** _____
  B _____

5 **A** _____
  B _____

6 **A** _____
  B _____

want and **would like** • In a restaurant
Food and drink • Going shopping

Thank you very much!

want and would like

1 Write sentences from the box.

> I'd like a stamp.
> I'd like to be a student again!
> I'd like to buy her new CD.
> ~~I'd like to have a big party.~~
> I'd like to see the new Stephen Spielberg film.
> I'd like to use your dictionary.

1 It's my birthday next week.

I'd like to have a big party.

2 I don't understand this word.

_____

3 I like that singer.

_____

4 I want to send this letter to France.

_____

5 I want to go to the cinema tonight.

_____

6 I don't like my job.

_____

2 [T 12.1] Write sentences.

1 a cup of tea
   I'd like a cup of tea, please.

2 change some traveller's cheques
   I'd like to change some traveller's cheques, please.

3 a glass of water
   _____

4 play chess
   _____

5 listen to a CD
   _____

6 a stamp
   _____

7 a cup of coffee
   _____

8 buy a computer
   _____

3 [T 12.2] Write questions.

1 a sandwich?
   Would you like a sandwich?

2 come to my party?
   Would you like to come to my party?

3 watch a video?
   _____

4 a glass of orange juice?
   _____

5 some cake?
   _____

6 go skiing?
   _____

7 a pizza?
   _____

8 play a computer game?
   _____

In a restaurant

Food and drink

4 Complete the words. Use *a, e, i, o,* and *u.*

1 ch **e** **e** s **e**   2 ch _ ck _ n   3 f _ sh   4 fr _ _ s   5 fr _ _ t

6 m _ n _ r _ l   7 s _ l _ d   8 s _ _ p   9 t _ m _ t _   10 v _ g _ t _ bl _ s
w _ t _ r

What would you like to eat?

5 Number the lines in the correct order.

Waiter

- [ ] And what would you like for your main course?
- [ ] Yes, of course. Thank you.
- [1] Are you ready to order?
- [ ] Certainly. A glass of white wine.
- [ ] The fish. Very good. And what would you like to drink?

Martha

- [ ] Can I have a glass of white wine, please?
- [ ] And I'd like a bottle of mineral water, too.
- [ ] Can I have the fish, please?
- [ ] Yes, er, I'd like the soup to start, please.

6 **T 12.3** Listen to the conversation. Look at the menu and tick ✓ the things Simon orders.

MENU

To start
seafood cocktail ☐
tomato soup ✓

Burgers
hamburger, salad, and fries ☐
cheeseburger, salad, and fries ☐

Sandwiches
ham ☐
chicken ☐
cheese ☐

Meat
steak and fries ☐
roast chicken and salad ☐

Side orders
fries ☐
mixed salad ☐

Desserts
ice-cream ☐
chocolate cake ☐
apple pie and cream ☐
fruit salad ☐

To drink
red wine ☐
white wine ☐
beer ☐
orange juice ☐
mineral water ☐
coffee ☐
tea ☐

7 Put the words in the correct order. Then use them to complete the conversation.

> cooked / like / would / How / you / it / ?
> main course / your / for / And / ?
> ~~to / you / Are / order / ready / ?~~
> glass / a / of / white / like / wine / I'd
> like / what / you / to start / would / ?
> I / roast / have / chicken / the / Can

Waiter (1) **Are you ready to order?**

Jane Yes, we are. Mike, (2) _____

Mike I'd like the seafood cocktail, please.

Jane And can I have tomato soup?

Waiter Certainly. (3) _____

Mike I'd like a steak, please.

Waiter (4) _____

Mike Medium.

Waiter Certainly. And for you?

Jane (5) _____ , please?

Waiter And what would you like to drink?

Jane (6) _____ , please.

Waiter Very good. And for you?

Mike Can I have a glass of mineral water, please?

Waiter Thank you.

8 Write a conversation in a restaurant. Use the menu in exercise 6.

Waiter _____

_____ _____
_____ _____
_____ _____
_____ _____
_____ _____
_____ _____
_____ _____
_____ _____
_____ _____
_____ _____
_____ _____
_____ _____

Pronunciation

9 T 12.4 **Which sound is different?**

1	it	(like)	live	him
2	thank	family	day	and
3	new	when	bed	went
4	drive	ride	I	sister
5	usually	my	family	February
6	post	go	shop	slowly
7	lunch	much	usually	but

Translation

10 **Write the sentences in your language.**

1 I'd like a cup of coffee, please.

_____

2 I'd like to buy a dictionary.

_____

3 'Would you like a glass of wine?'
  'Yes, please.'

_____

4 I want to send an email.

_____

5 What would you like to do this evening?

_____

Reading

You are what you eat …

11 **Read the four texts. Answer the questions. Write the names.**

Hi, I'm Jake. I'm from Manchester. I love cooking. Every Friday evening I cook a meal at home for my friends. I eat lots of fresh food – fish, vegetables, and fruit – but I like pies and cakes, too. I hate junk food!

Hello. I'm Helga. I'm German. I never eat meat or fish – I'm vegetarian. I only eat vegetables and fruit. I sometimes go out for a meal with friends. There are a lot of good vegetarian restaurants in Berlin.

1 Who loves cooking?   _Jake_

2 Who goes to a bar in the evening with friends?   _____

3 Who doesn't eat meat?   _____

4 Who loves junk food?   _____

Hi, I'm Mitsuo. I'm a businessman and I live in Tokyo. I usually finish work at seven o'clock in the evening. Then I go out with my friends to a bar near the office. We usually have chicken or fish and we drink beer or 'sake' – Japanese wine.

Hi, I'm Serena. I'm from Los Angeles. I always have a burger and fries for lunch, and a bottle of Coke. In the evening my mum cooks a big meal – meat and vegetables. But I only eat the meat.

5 Who sometimes goes out for a meal with friends? _____

6 Who eats lots of vegetables, fruit, and fish? _____

7 Who only eats meat for dinner? _____

8 Who drinks beer? _____

Everyday English

Going shopping

12 **T 12.5** Listen to the six conversations. Where are the people? Tick ✓ the places.

	1	2	3	4	5	6
In the street						
In a clothes shop	✓					
At the market						
In a newsagent						

13 Complete the conversations. Use the words in the box.

> Do you sell   in a size 44   No, thanks
> that's all   The changing rooms   try on
> two kilos of   ~~Where can I buy~~   Next to

1 A Excuse me. **Where can I buy** a phone card?

   B In a newsagent.

   A Is there a newsagent near here?

   B Yes, a hundred metres from here. _____ the church.

2 A Can I help you ?

   B _____ . I'm just looking.

3 A Excuse me. Do you have this jumper _____ ?

   B No, I'm sorry . That's all we have.

4 A I'd like to _____ this T-shirt, please.

   B Sure. What size are you?

   A I think I'm a thirty-eight.

   B Fine. _____ are over there.

5 A Yes, madam. What would you like?

   B I'd like _____ apples, please.

   A Anything else?

   B No, _____ , thanks. How much is that?

6 A Excuse me. _____ pens?

   B No, I'm sorry. I don't.

   A Where can I buy them?

   B Try the newsagent.

13

Colours • Present Continuous • Present Simple and
Present Continuous • Clothes • What's the matter?

Colours

1 **T 13.1** Write the colours.

| black | blue | brown | green |
| grey | red | white | ~~yellow~~ |

1 yellow
2 _____
3 _____
4 _____
5 _____
6 _____
7 _____
8 _____

Present Continuous

2 Write the -*ing* forms.

1	wash	washing
2	swim	swimming
3	drive	driving
4	study	_____
5	run	_____
6	make	_____
7	sit	_____
8	watch	_____
9	phone	_____
10	eat	_____

3 Write sentences.

1 He / read / a magazine
   He's reading a magazine.

2 I / learn / English

   _____

3 We / sit / in the living room

   _____

4 She / talk / to her sister

   _____

5 They / enjoy / the film

   _____

6 He / dance

   _____

7 I / work / at home

   _____

4 Write negative and positive sentences.

1 We usually play football in the evening, but today **we aren't playing** football. **We're playing** tennis.

2 They usually drink wine with their dinner. But today
_____ wine.
_____ beer.

3 He usually sits next to Marco in class. But today
_____ next to Marco.
_____ next to Maria.

4 I usually have lunch in the office. But today
_____ lunch in the office.
_____ lunch in a café.

5 She usually walks to school. But this morning
_____ to school.
_____ to school.

6 You usually wear a jacket to work. But today
_____ a jacket.
_____ a T-shirt and jeans!

5 **T 13.2** Look at the picture. Write questions and answers.

1 Elena / listen to music?

 A Is Elena listening to music?

 B Yes, she is.

2 Paul and Pascal / play tennis?

 A Are Paul and Pascal playing tennis?

 B No, they aren't. They're playing football.

3 Elena / read a book?

 A _____

 B _____

4 Pascal and Paul / wear T-shirts?

 A _____

 B _____

5 Roberto / sit / on the beach?

 A _____

 B _____

6 Roberto and Elena / swim?

 A _____

 B _____

7 Elena / drink / Coca-Cola?

 A _____

 B _____

8 Roberto / read a magazine?

 A _____

 B _____

Present Simple and Present Continuous

6 Complete the sentences. Use *am, is, are, do,* and *does.*

1 '**Do** you like pizza?' 'Yes, I **do** .'

2 'What _____ you doing?' 'I _____ reading.'

3 '_____ she drive to work?' 'No, she walks.'

4 'Where _____ you live?' 'In London.'

5 Look! He _____ wearing yellow trousers!

6 '_____ he like skiing?' 'Yes, he _____ ?'

7 Complete the sentences. Use *'m not, isn't, aren't, don't,* and *doesn't.*

1 George **doesn't** like vegetables.

2 This film is terrible! We _____ enjoying it.

3 'Is Luke cooking dinner?' 'No, he _____ ?'

4 They _____ go out in the evening. They always stay at home.

5 I _____ going to work today because it's Sunday.

6 She has a dog, but she _____ have a cat.

Translation

8 Write the sentences in your language.

1 He's learning English.

 _____

 _____

2 You aren't listening to me!

 _____

 _____

3 What are you wearing today?

 _____

 _____

4 What do you wear at weekends?

 _____

 _____

5 They usually work in the evening, but this evening they're watching TV.

 _____

 _____

Reading

Summer in Portugal

9 Read the postcard and answer the questions.

1 Where are Lisa and Paul?
   They're in Albufeira.

2 What's Paul doing?

   _____

3 What's the weather like?

   _____

4 Where do they usually stay?

   _____

5 Where are they staying this year?

   _____

6 What do Lisa and Paul do every morning?

   _____

Dear Carol,
We're having a great time in Albufeira. We're sitting in a café near the beach. Paul's reading the newspaper and I'm writing this postcard to you! The sun's shining and it's really hot.

We come to Portugal every summer. We usually stay with my friends Ana and Zé, but this year we're in a hotel because Ana's parents are staying with them.

The beaches here are fantastic. We go swimming every morning. Did you enjoy your holiday in America?
See you soon.
        Love,
            Lisa and Paul

Carol Miller

24 Clinton Road

Edinburgh   EH9 2AW

Scotland

ALBUFEIRA, PORTUGAL

Vocabulary

Clothes

10 **T 13.3** What are the clothes?

1 toosb **boots**
2 strouesr _____
3 tsshor _____
4 taoc _____
5 intraers _____
6 umpjer _____
7 sdres _____
8 riskt _____
9 sanldsa _____
10 hirts _____
11 oeshs _____
12 jaetck _____
13 tha _____

11 **T 13.4** Listen and look at the pictures. Who is it? Write the letters.

1 **a**   3 ____   5 ____   7 ____
2 ____   4 ____   6 ____   8 ____

12 Look at the pictures. Describe Mike and Carol's clothes.

Mike

1 _____
  _____
  _____
  _____
  _____

Carol

2 _____
  _____
  _____
  _____
  _____
  _____

13 What are you wearing? What colours are your clothes?

_____
_____
_____
_____
_____

Everyday English

What's the matter?

14 [T 13.5] Match the words and pictures.

| cold | hot | hungry | bored | thirsty | ~~tired~~ |

1 tired

2 _____

3 _____

4 _____

5 _____

6 _____

15 Match a line in A with a line in B.

A	B
1 I'm hungry.	a Why don't you have a drink?
2 I'm thirsty.	b Why don't you put on your coat?
3 I'm hot.	c Why don't you sit down and relax?
4 I'm cold.	d Why don't you have a sandwich?
5 I'm bored.	e Why don't you go to the cinema?
6 I'm tired.	f Why don't you go for a swim?

Present Continuous for future
Transport and travel · Going sightseeing

It's time to go!

Present Continuous for future

1 Look at Charlie's diary for next week. Write sentences about his plans.

> **APRIL**
>
> **Monday**
> 2.00 p.m. meet Jim
> 7.00 p.m. go to the cinema with Jane
>
> **Tuesday**
> 10.00 a.m. see the dentist
> 2.00 p.m. play football
>
> **Wednesday**
> 9.00 a.m. drive to Liverpool
> p.m. visit Uncle Joseph

1 <u>On Monday afternoon he's meeting Jim.</u>
2 _____
3 _____
4 _____
5 _____
6 _____

2 Which sentences describe the present? Which sentences describe the future? Write *P* or *F*.

1 I**'m going** to the cinema tomorrow evening. **F**
2 Look! He**'s wearing** a red and green shirt. **P**
3 What **are** you **doing** tomorrow? ___
4 I**'m** really **enjoying** this meal. The fish is delicious! ___
5 Where **are** you **going** on Tuesday? ___
6 'What's the weather like?' 'The sun**'s shining**, but it's a bit cold.' ___
7 'Where's Joe?' 'He**'s watching** TV in the living room.' ___
8 Next weekend they**'re staying** at home.' ___

3 Write questions and answers about Joanna's plans for next Friday.

> **Friday**
> – 8.30 a.m. train to London
>   meet Sophie at Paddington Station
> – 1.00 p.m. train to Cambridge to see Mike
> – 5.00 p.m. go back to Oxford
>   go to bed early
>
> **Saturday**

1 where / go / Friday morning?
  A <u>Where's Joanna going on Friday morning?</u>
  B <u>She's going to London.</u>
2 how / travel?
  A _____
  B _____
3 who / meet?
  A _____
  B _____
4 where / meet / her?
  A _____
  B _____
5 when / go / to Cambridge?
  A _____
  B _____
6 why / go / to Cambridge?
  A _____
  B _____
7 what / do / Friday evening?
  A _____
  B _____

Listening

Hannah's diary

4 **T 14.1** Look at Hannah's diary for next week. Listen to the four phone conversations and complete her diary.

Conversation 1: with Pete
Conversation 2: with Lisa
Conversation 3: with Jack
Conversation 4: with Tina

MONDAY

TUESDAY

WEDNESDAY
2.00 p.m. see the dentist

THURSDAY

FRIDAY

Pronunciation

5 **T 14.2** Listen and repeat.

'<u>What's</u> your <u>name</u>?'
'<u>Mark</u>. What's <u>your</u> name?'

'<u>Where</u> do you <u>live</u>?'
'In <u>Paris</u>. Where do <u>you</u> live?'

6 **T 14.3** Underline the stressed words in these conversations. Then listen and check.

1 'What's your job?'
   'I'm a doctor. What's your job?'

2 'What would you like?'
   'A coffee. What would you like?'

3 'Where do you work?
   'In Rome. Where do you work?'

4 'Where are you from?'
   'Prague. Where are you from?'

Translation

7 Write the sentences in your language.

1 I'm going to Rome tomorrow.

_____

2 How long are you staying there?

_____

3 What are you doing on Friday evening?

_____

4 'Where's Ian?' 'He's playing football.'

_____

Vocabulary

Transport and travel

8 Label the pictures.

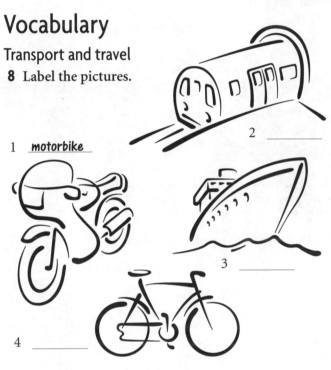

1 <u>motorbike</u>

2 _____

3 _____

4 _____

9 Complete the text. Use the words in the box.

| arrived | ~~booked~~ | caught |
| collected | had | packed | went |

Last week we decided to go to Paris for the weekend.
We phoned the travel agent on Thursday and
(1) **booked** the flights and hotel. In the evening we
(2) _____ our bags and on Friday morning I
(3) _____ the tickets from the travel agent. We
drove to the airport on Friday evening and
(4) _____ the plane at 7.30. We (5) _____ at
the hotel at 9.30. On Saturday and Sunday we
(6) _____ sightseeing in Paris and we came back on
Sunday evening. We (7) _____ a great time!

Reading and listening

The Smiths

10 **T 14.4** Read and listen to the text. Put the pictures in the correct order.

Where's our car!?

Last Saturday John and Vanessa Smith visited Amsterdam. They went by car. They left their car in a street near a canal. Then they went sightseeing. At four o'clock they decided to go back to their car. But where was it? They forgot the name of the street! They looked for the car for four hours and then went to the police.

The Smiths

'We can't find our car,' said Mr Smith to the police officer.

'Where did you leave it?' asked the officer.

'Er … near a canal, I think,' said Mr Smith.

'But there are lots of canals in Amsterdam, Mr Smith … '

Mr and Mrs Smith stayed in Amsterdam for five days, but they didn't find their car. On Wednesday they caught the plane back to London. A week later the police in Amsterdam phoned the Smiths.

'We found your car today,' the officer said. 'Would you like to collect it?'

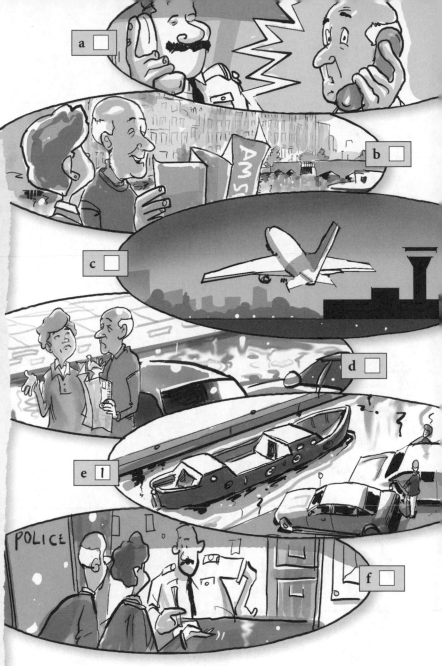

A canal in Amsterdam

11 Answer the questions about the text.

1 How did the Smiths travel to Amsterdam?
   They went by car.

2 Where did they leave their car?
   _____

3 How long did they stay in Amsterdam?
   _____

4 Did they find their car?
   _____

5 How did they get back to London?
   _____

6 When did the police find their car?
   _____

Everyday English

Going sightseeing

12 Match a line in A with a line in B.

A	B
1 I'd like a map of the town, please.	a It goes from the bus station in George Street.
2 Where does the bus go from?	b From ten thirty to six every day.
3 When is the church open?	c £4 for adults and £2 for children.
4 How much is it to get in?	d Here you are.

13 **T 14.5** Listen and complete the posters.

❷

Science Museum

Open from _____
to _____ every day.
Adults _____
Children _____

❶

Open from ....
to ....
Adults ....
Children ....

PRINCE CHARLES PARK
ZOO

BUS TOUR
OF THE CITY

The bus leaves at 9.00, 11.00 _____ and 3.00 from Queen Street. The tour takes _____ hours.

SEEING TOUR

❸

WESTMINSTER ABBEY

Tapescripts

Unit 1

T 1.1

1 A Hello. My name's Stefano Gentile. What's your name?
   B My name's Juan Alonso.
   A Hello, Juan.
2 A Karl, this is Maria. Maria, this is Karl.
   B Hello, Karl.
   A Hello, Maria.
3 B Hello. I'm Susan Brown. What's your name?
   A Christophe Martignac.
   B Hello, Christophe.
4 B Hi, Martin. How are you?
   A OK, thanks, Sally. And you?
   B I'm very well, thanks.

T 1.5

1 six	4 nine	7 ten
2 three	5 seven	8 two
3 one	6 five	

Unit 2

T 2.5

Hello, my name is Carmen. I'm a doctor and I'm from Madrid, in Spain.
I'm in London. This is a photograph of my school. It's in the centre of London. I'm in the photograph, and my teacher is in the photograph, too. His name is Andrew. He's from Scotland.

T 2.7

1 sixteen	6 fifteen
2 eleven	7 twelve
3 twenty-seven	8 twenty-nine
4 thirteen	9 twenty
5 thirty	10 eighteen

Unit 3

T 3.7

I = Interviewer   K = Kirsty

I Hello.
K Hi.
I What's your name, please?
K Kirsty. Kirsty Logan.
I Kirsty Logan. Thanks. And how old are you, Kirsty?
K I'm 18.
I 18. OK. Now, are you a student?
K No, I'm not.
I Oh? What's your job?
K I'm a shop assistant.
I Uh, huh. You aren't married, are you?
K No, I'm not.
I Are you from England, Kirsty?
K Well, no. I'm not from England. I'm from Scotland.
I Ah, Scotland. OK, where in Scotland?
K Perth.
I Perth. Thanks. Now, what's your address?
K 43 King Street.
I 43 King Street. And your phone number?
K 417 8924.
I 417 85–
K No, 417 8924.
I 417 8924. Good. Thank you very much, Kirsty.

Unit 4

T 4.2

Hi. My name's Winston. I'm 30 and I'm a restaurant manager. My wife's name is Carol. She's 29 and she's a teacher. We're from Oxford in England. This is a photo of our family.
Our children are Robert and Jessica. Robert's five and his sister is six. Their school is in Oxford.
Carol's parents are in the photo too. Her father is a police officer, and her mother's a shop assistant.

T 4.7

1 teacher	4 husband	7 wife
2 Brazil	5 daughter	
3 family	6 photograph	

Unit 5

T 5.4

P = Paolo   S = Susan

P Hello. I'm Paolo.
S Hi, Paolo. I'm Susan. Where do you come from, Paolo?
P I'm from Italy, but I live here in Bristol.
S Really?
P Yes, I work in a bank.
S Do you like Bristol?
P Yes, I do. It's great. Do you live in Bristol?
S No, I don't. I live in London.
P What's your job?
S I'm a restaurant manager.
P A restaurant manager? Really?
S Yes, I have a restaurant in Chelsea.
P Oh, I don't like English food very much.
S But the food in my restaurant isn't English. It's Italian!
P Oh!

T 5.7

1 £3.79	4 84p	7 50p
2 59p	5 £28.10	8 £19.23
3 £49.99	6 £62.45	

T 5.8

1 How much is the wine?
   It's £6.75.
2 How much is the camera?
   It's £87.50.
3 How much is the dictionary?
   It's £11.30.
4 How much is the pizza?
   It's £3.65.
5 How much is the hamburger?
   It's £1.95.
6 How much is the mobile phone?
   It's £99.99.
7 How much is the ice-cream?
   It's 80p.
8 How much is the bag?
   It's £32.49.

Unit 6

T 6.1

1 A What time is it, please?
   B It's two fifteen.
   A Thank you.
2 A What time is it, please?
   B It's eleven o'clock.
   A Thank you.
3 A What time is it, please?
   B It's ten thirty.
   A Thank you.
4 A What time is it, please?
   B It's four forty-five.
   A Thank you.
5 A What time is it, please?
   B It's one fifteen.
   A Thank you.
6 A What time is it, please?
   B It's three forty-five.
   A Thank you.

T 6.4

Anna is a nurse. She works in a hospital in Dublin. She usually goes to work at ten o'clock in the evening. At six fifteen in the morning, she leaves work. She goes home by bus, then has breakfast and a shower. She goes to bed at seven thirty and gets up at three in the afternoon. She has lunch at three thirty and then goes shopping. Sometimes she goes for a walk. She has dinner at eight thirty. Then she usually listens to music or watches television. She goes to work again at ten o'clock.

Unit 7

C = Chat show host   D = Dan Brat

C I'm with Dan Brat, the famous Hollywood star. Hello, Dan.
D Hi.
C Where do you live, Dan? Here, in Hollywood?
D I sometimes live in Hollywood. Sometimes in New York, sometimes in Hawaii …
C How many houses do you have?
D Um, five. I have five houses. And I love them all. But my favourite house is in Hawaii.
C Why do you like Hawaii, Dan?
D Because it's beautiful, it's fantastic. I love it.
C Mmm. And you're married to Billy-Jo Davies.
D Yeah. Billy-Jo's my wife. She's wife number five.
C Number five? And, er, she's a film star, too.
D That's right.
C Do you work with her?
D No, we never work together.
C When do you see Billy-Jo?
D I sometimes see her in the evening – on television! I love her movies!
C And how many children have you got, Dan?
D Um, six. No, seven. Or is it eight? No, it's seven.
C OK! Thank you very much. Dan Brat!

T 7.5

1 **A** Can I try on this jacket, please?
  B Of course. The changing rooms are just here.
2 **A** Can I have a ticket to London, please?
  B Sure. Single or return?
  A Single, please.
  B That's £15, please.
  A There you are.
  B Thank you. £20. Here's your ticket and £5 change.
3 **A** Can I send an email, please?
  B OK. PC Number 15.
  A How much is it?
  B 1p a minute. Pay at the end, please.
4 **A** Good afternoon. Can I help you?
  B Yes, can I change this traveller's cheque, please?
  A Of course. How much is it?
  B £50.
5 **A** Can I have a pizza, please?
  B There you are.
  A How much is it?
  B £2.30.
  A Thank you.
  B £5. Here's £2.70 change.

Unit 8

T 8.7

There's a computer on the table.
There's an armchair next to the table.
There's a bag under the table, and a magazine in the bag.
There are two pictures on the wall.
There's a cat on the armchair.
There are two CDs on the floor next to the armchair.
There's a phone on a small table next to the lamp.
There's a photograph on the table, too, next to the phone.

T 8.9

1 Start from the Chinese restaurant.
  Go down Church Street. Turn right into Park Street. It's on the left.
2 Start from the theatre.
  Go down Park Street. Turn right into Station Road. Then turn right into Queen Street. It's on the right, next to the bank.
3 Start from the chemist.
  Go down Station Road. Turn left into King's Road. It's on the left next to the cinema.
4 Start from the railway station.
  Go down Station Road, past Park Street. Turn right into Oxford Road. Turn left at the Chinese restaurant into Church Street. Go past King's Road. It's on the left.
5 Start from the Internet café.
  Go down London Road. Turn left into Park Street. Go past the theatre. It's on the left.

Unit 9

T 9.1

1 two thousand and five
2 nineteen seventy-six
3 fifteen eighty-eight
4 nineteen fourteen
5 two thousand and three
6 seventeen fifty
7 eighteen sixty-two
8 nineteen ninety-five

T 9.2

This is my family. My grandparents are Alberto and Maria. They live with us, in Milan. They were both born in 1930.

My parents are Roberto and Sofia. My dad was born in Rome in 1955. My mum was born in 1957 in Florence. I was born in 1980. I have a brother, Alessandro. He was born in 1978.

My uncle Luigi – he's my dad's brother – he was born in 1957 and his wife, Rosa, was born in 1959. They have two daughters: Arianna and Donatella. They're my cousins and they were born in April 1985.

I also have an aunt, Antonella. She's my dad's little sister. She was born in 1959. She's married. Her husband's name is Marco, and he was born in 1960. They don't have any children.

T 9.6

1 the third of January
2 the fifteen of July
3 the twenty-second of March
4 the twelfth of November
5 the twenty-eighth of February
6 the fifth of June
7 the eleventh of September
8 the thirty-first of December
9 the sixth of April
10 the nineteenth of August
11 the seventeenth of May
12 the tenth of October
13 the first of March

Unit 10

T 10.2

Yesterday was Saturday. I got up at seven o'clock and had breakfast. I went to work at eight thirty. I'm a doctor, so I sometimes work on Saturday morning. I worked until 12.30. After work, I had lunch with some friends in a restaurant. Then we went to the cinema. We saw 'Gladiator'. It's a fantastic film! After that, I went home. In the evening I stayed at home. I cooked dinner, then listened to music. At ten o'clock I had a shower and went to bed.

T 10.5

R = Receptionist   B = Boris

R Good evening. Can I help you?
B Um, yes. Can I join the sports centre, please?
R Certainly. What's your name?
B Boris Wehr.
R How do you spell Wehr?
B W–E–H–R.
R And where do you live, Mr Wehr?
B 26 London Road … Oxford.
R And do you know the postcode?
B Yes, it's OX3 … 8EF.
R OX3 8EF. Thanks. And what's the phone number?
B 01865 926841.
R 01865 926841.
B That's right.
R And what's your date of birth?
B Date of …? Sorry, I don't understand.
R Your date of birth. When were you born?
B Oh, 1st February, 1985.
R 1st February, 1985. And where are you from?
B Germany.
R Germany. OK. And what sports are you interested in?
B Squash and fitness training.
R Thanks. Can you sign here, please?

Unit 11

T 11.5

M = Mike   L = Lisa

M So, Lisa, why do you want to be in our pop group, *Raincloud*?
L Because I love your music. I have all your CDs. They're brilliant.
M And you can play the guitar?
L Yes, I can. And I can play the piano.
M Yeah? That's good. And can you read music?
L Um, yes, but not very well.
M I see. Now, we sometimes give concerts in other countries. Last year we were on tour in France. We usually go by car. Can you drive?
L Uh, no, I can't. But I can speak French. My mum's French, you see.
M That's good. And can you speak German?
L I can understand German, but I can't speak it very well.
M OK, Lisa, can you play the guitar for us now?
L Sure.

T 11.7

1 I can draw.
2 We can't swim.
3 Can you ski?
4 Yes, I can.
5 She can't cook.
6 Can they drive?
7 Yes, they can.

Unit 12

T 12.3

W = Waitress   S = Simon

W Are you ready to order?
S Yes, I am.
W What would you like to start?
S Can I have the tomato soup, please?
W Tomato soup. Certainly. And for your main course?
S I'd like the roast chicken, please. And can I have a side order of fries?
W Certainly. Roast chicken and salad with a side order of fries. And would you like a dessert?
S Yes, I'd like apple pie and cream, please.
W Very good. What would you like to drink?
S Can I have a beer, please?
W Certainly.
S And a coffee with my dessert, please.
W Thank you very much.

T 12.5

1 **A** Excuse me. Do you have this shirt in a medium?
  B No, I'm sorry. That's all we have.
2 **A** Excuse me. Do you sell computer magazines?
  B Yes, we do. They're over there.
3 **A** Excuse me. Where can I buy some tomatoes?
  B At the market.

A Where is there a market?
B Three hundred yards from here. Go straight on and turn left at the church.
4 **A** I'd like to try on this T-shirt, please.
  B Certainly. The changing rooms are over there.
5 **A** Yes, madam. Can I help you?
  B Yes, I'd like some potatoes please. Three kilos.
  A Three kilos of potatoes … anything else?
  B No, that's all, thank you.
  A That's £1.80, please.
6 **A** Can I help you?
  B Yes, do you sell fruit juice?
  A Yes, we do – over there next to the magazines and newspapers.
  B Oh, yes. Thanks.

Unit 13

T 13.4

1 She's wearing a skirt and shoes.
2 She's wearing a jumper and a coat.
3 She's wearing a skirt and sandals.
4 She's wearing trousers and boots.
5 She's wearing a dress and a hat.
6 She's wearing a shirt, a jacket, and a skirt.
7 She's wearing a shirt, a jumper, and a skirt.
8 She's wearing a coat, a hat, and shoes.

Unit 14

T 14.1

H = Hannah   P = Pete

1 **H** 202567. Hello.
  P Hi, Hannah. It's Pete here.
  H Oh, hello, Pete. How are you?
  P Fine, fine. Listen. What are you doing on Monday evening?
  H Monday evening? Er … nothing.
  P Well, would you like to go out for a meal?
  H Yes, great idea. What time?
  P Eight o'clock?
  H Fine.
  P OK. See you on Monday at eight. Bye.
  H Bye.

H = Hannah   L = Lisa

2 **H** 202567. Hello.
  L Hello. Is that Hannah?
  H Yes. Hi, Lisa.
  L Hi! Listen, I'm going to the cinema on Tuesday evening with Mark. Would you like to come with us?
  H What are you going to see?
  L 'Captain Corelli's Mandolin'.
  H Yes, I'd really like to see it. What time does it start?
  L Nine o'clock, but I'm meeting Mark at the cinema at eight thirty.
  H OK, see you at the cinema at eight thirty.
  L Great! Bye!
  H Bye.

H = Hannah   J = Jack

3 **H** 202567. Hello.
  J Hi, Hannah. It's Jack.
  H Hello, Jack.
  J How are you?
  H I'm fine.
  J Are you doing anything on Wednesday afternoon?
  H Um, yes, I'm seeing the dentist.
  J Oh, well, what are doing on Thursday afternoon?
  H Nothing.
  J Would you like to play tennis?
  H Oh, yes, I'd love to!
  H OK. Let's play on Thursday afternoon, at … er … two o'clock?
  J Two o'clock is fine.

H = Hannah   T = Tina

4 **H** 202567. Hello.
  T Hi, It's Tina. Hannah, would you like to go shopping in London next week?
  H That's a great idea. When would you like to go?
  T Well, I'm not doing anything on Thursday.
  H Oh, I'm playing tennis with Jack on Thursday afternoon.
  T Well, what about Wednesday?
  H No, I'm seeing the dentist!
  T Friday?
  H Yes, Friday's fine. Let's meet at the station at nine thirty. There's a train at ten.
  T OK. See you there.
  H See you there. Bye.

T 14.5

C = Clerk   T = Tourist

1 **C** Good morning. Can I help you?
  T Yes, we'd like to visit the zoo. Er, where is it?
  C It's in Prince Charles Park.
  T And when is it open?
  C From ten o'clock to four o'clock every day.
  T And is it expensive? How much is it to get in?
  C It's £8 for adults and £4 for children.
  T Thanks.

2 **C** Can I help you?
  T Yes, er, we'd like to visit the Science Museum. When is it open?
  C From nine thirty to six o'clock.
  T And how much is it to get in?
  C It's £5 for adults and £3 for children.
  T Thanks.

3 **T** Hello. I'd like to go on a bus tour of the city. Where does the bus leave from?
  C It goes from Queen Street, and the tour takes two hours.
  T When does the next bus leave?
  C It's twelve thirty now, so the next bus leaves at … er … one o'clock.
  T Thanks very much.

Workbook key

Unit 1

1 1 2, 3, 1
2 4, 2, 1, 3

2 2 Very well, thanks.
3 This is James.
4 What's your name?
5 My name's Raquel.

3 2 c 3 a 4 b

4 1 **Pierre Dupont** Hello. My name's
Pierre Dupont. What's your *name*?
Alicia González Alicia. Alicia
González.

2 **Pierre** Hello, Alicia. *How* are you?
Alicia *Fine/OK* , thanks. And *you*?
Pierre Very *well, thanks* .

3 **Alicia** Pierre, this is Aya Saito.
Aya, *this is* Pierre Dupont.
Aya Saito Hello, Pierre.
Pierre *Hello*, Aya.

5 1 **Klaus Fischer** Hello. My name's
Klaus Fischer. What's your name?
Denise Minjon Denise. Denise
Minjon.

2 **Denise** Hello, Klaus. How are you?
Klaus Very well, thanks. And you?
Denise Fine, thanks.

3 **Klaus** Denise, this is Paolo Silvetti.
Paolo, this is Denise Minjon.
Paolo Silvetti Hello, Denise.
Denise Hello, Paolo.

7 2 It's a house.
3 It's a car.
4 It's a hamburger.
5 It's a book.
6 It's a sandwich.
7 It's a camera.
8 It's a television.
9 It's a bag.
10 It's a computer.

9 2 seven 3 ten 4 six 5 one
6 five 7 two 8 three 9 four
10 nine, nine, nine

10 2 5 3 9 4 1 5 2 6 8 7 6
8 4 9 7 10 10

11 2 3 3 1 4 9 5 7 6 5
7 10 8 2

12 2 s 3 s 4 s 5 es 6 s
7 s 8 s 9 s 10 s

13 2 nine books 3 ten bags 4 one
computer 5 two televisions 6 three
houses 7 six photographs 8 seven
sandwiches 9 eight hamburgers
10 four cameras

Unit 2

1 2 The United States 3 Japan
4 France 5 Spain 6 Australia
7 Italy 8 England

2 2 France 3 Spain 4 Italy
5 The United States 6 Japan
7 Australia 8 Brazil

3 A France B England C Japan
D Italy E Australia

4 2 Where's Boston?
It's in the United States.
3 Where's Oxford?
It's in England.
4 Where's Milan?
It's in Italy.
5 Where's Paris?
It's in France.
6 Where's Rio de Janeiro?
It's in Brazil.
7 Where's Sydney?
It's in Australia.
8 Where's Tokyo?
It's in Japan.

5 2 Scotland 3 Wales 4 England

6 2 What's *her* name?
Her name's *Amy*.
Where's *she* from?
She's from *the United States*.
3 What's *his* name?
His name's *Luis*.
Where's *he* from?
He's from *Brazil*.
4 *What's her* name?
Her name's Junko.
Where's she from?
She's from *Japan*.
5 What's his name?
His name's Steven.
Where's he from?
He's from Australia.
6 What's her name?
Her name's Denise.
Where's she from?
She's from France.

7 1 **Henri** Hello. My name's Henri.
What's your name?
Isabel Isabel.
Henri Where *are you from*, Isabel?
Isabel Coimbra, in Portugal. Where
are you from?
Henri *I'm* from Paris.

2 **Henri** *Hello*, Isabel. *How* are you?
Isabel *Fine*, thanks. And *you*?
Henri Very well, *thanks*. Isabel, *this* is
Ana. *She's from* Portugal.
Isabel *Hello*, Ana.
Ana *Hello*, Isabel. *Where* are you *from*?
Isabel *I'm from* Coimbra.
Ana Oh, *I'm from* Coimbra, *too*!

9 2 Italy 3 computer programmer
4 married 5 France 6 teacher
7 Jean-Claude 8 Japan 9 doctor
10 hospital

10 2 She's from   3 her school
   4 London   5 Andrew   6 Scotland

13 11 eleven   12 twelve   13 thirteen
   14 fourteen   15 fifteen   16 sixteen
   17 seventeen   18 eighteen   19 nineteen
   20 twenty   21 twenty-one
   22 twenty-two   23 twenty-three
   24 twenty-four   25 twenty-five
   26 twenty-six   27 twenty-seven
   28 twenty-eight   29 twenty-nine
   30 thirty

14 2 twenty-nine   3 twelve   4 fifteen
   5 twenty   6 seventeen   7 eleven
   8 thirty   9 twenty-seven   10 twenty-one

15 2 twenty-eight   3 eighteen
   4 thirteen   5 twenty-three   6 sixteen
   7 twenty-four   8 nineteen
   9 twenty-six   10 twenty-five

16 2 11   3 27   4 13   5 30   6 15
   7 12   8 29   9 20   10 18

Unit 3

1 2 businessman
   3 doctor
   4 nurse
   5 police officer
   6 shop assistant
   7 student
   8 teacher

2 3 What's his job?
   He's a taxi driver.
   4 What's her job?
   She's a teacher.
   5 What's his job?
   He's a businessman.
   6 What's her job?
   She's a doctor.
   7 What's his job?
   He's a shop assistant.
   8 What's her job?
   She's a student.

3 2 She isn't a doctor.
   She's a nurse.
   3 He isn't a businessman.
   He's a police officer.
   4 She isn't a taxi driver.
   She's a shop assistant.

4 Country
   Address
   Phone number
   Age
   Job
   Married?

5 2 Where's she from?
   3 What's her address?
   4 What's her phone number?
   5 How old is she?
   6 What's her job?
   7 Is she married?

6 2 No, she isn't.   3 Yes, she is.
   4 No, she isn't.   5 Yes, she is.
   6 No, she isn't.   7 Yes, she is.
   8 Yes, she is.

7 All answers: Yes, I am. / No, I'm not.

8 2 Where are you from?
   3 What's your address?
   4 What's your phone number?
   5 How old are you?
   6 What's your job?
   7 Are you married?

12 A car, fine, nurse
   B doctor, student, number, sandwich
   C hospital, officer, Portugal, hamburger

13 Age *18*
   Job *Shop assistant*
   Married? *No*
   Country *Scotland*
   Address *43 King Street*
   Phone number *417 8924*

14 2 No, she isn't.   3 Yes, she is.
   4 No, she isn't.   5 Yes, she is.
   6 No, she isn't.   7 No, it isn't.

15 1 They're from the United States.
   2 No, they aren't. (Michael is from
      Canada and Carlos is from Cuba.)
   3 They're in London, England.
   4 They're 22.
   5 No, he isn't. (He's 24.)

16 2 Good morning.   3 Good afternoon.
   4 Good evening.   5 Good night.

17 2 Good evening.   3 Good morning.
   4 Good afternoon.   5 Good morning.
   6 Good evening.   7 Good afternoon.

18 2 Oh, thanks.   3 Pardon?   4 Sorry!
   5 I don't know.

Unit 4

1 3 ✓
   4 ✗ Edward is Andrew's brother.
   5 ✓
   6 ✗ Elizabeth is Andrew's mother.
   7 ✓
   8 ✓
   9 ✗ Anne is Philip's daughter.

2 2 parents
   3 brother
   4 mother
   5 wife
   6 children
   7 sister
   8 father
   9 daughter
   10 husband

3 2 This is Susan's camera.
   3 This is Francesca's house.
   4 This is Anita's bag.
   5 This is Fabien's computer.
   6 This is Frank's dictionary.
   7 This is Akiko's car.
   8 This is David's dog.

4 3 is   4 P   5 P   6 is
   7 is   8 P   9 P   10 P

5 4 's   5 's   6 s   7 's   8 's
   9 ✗   10 's

6 you   *your*
   he   *his*
   she   *her*
   we   *our*
   they   *their*

7 2 your   3 their   4 Her
   5 My   6 his   7 Our

8 2 restaurant manager   3 Carol
   4 29   5 teacher   6 6   7 school
   8 police officer

9 **Jobs:** doctor, nurse, businessman, teacher
   Countries: Brazil, Japan, Spain
   Numbers: nineteen, twelve, six,
      twenty-three
   Families: father, wife, son, sister

11 A son, wife, France
   B daughter, children, husband
   C Brazil, hello
   D family, businessman, manager

13 2 have   3 have   4 has
   5 has   6 have   7 has

15 2 He's 57.
  3 Her name's Catherine Zeta-Jones.
  4 She's from Wales.
  5 They're actors.
  6 His name's Dylan.
  7 He's two.
  8 It's on 25th September.

16 /eɪ/ /i:/ /e/ /aɪ/ /əʊ/ /u:/ /ɑ:/

a	b	f	i	o	q	r
h	c	l	y			u
j	d	m				w
k	e	n				
	g	s				
	p	x				
	t	z				
	v					

17 2 Brazil 3 family 4 husband
  5 daughter 6 photograph 7 wife

18 2 And your name is?
  3 How do you spell your surname?
  4 Thank you. I'm sorry. He isn't in his office. What's your phone number?
  5 Thank you for telephoning. Goodbye.

Unit 5

1 **Sports:** 2 swimming 3 skiing
  4 tennis
  Food: 5 Chinese food 6 hamburgers
  7 ice-cream 8 Italian food 9 pizza
  10 oranges
  Drinks: 11 tea 12 beer
  13 coffee 14 wine 15 Coca-Cola

3 3 No, I don't. 4 Yes, I do. 5 Yes, I do.
  6 No, I don't. 7 No, I don't. 8 Yes, I do.

5 3 Yes, they do.
  4 No, they don't. They speak English and French.
  5 No, they don't. They live in the country, near Oviedo.
  6 Yes, they do.
  7 Yes, they do.
  8 No, they don't. They like football and skiing.

6 2 Do you like Chinese food?
  3 Where do you work?
  4 Do you drink coffee?
  5 What sports do you like?
  6 How many languages do you speak?

8 2 Do they have a dog?
  3 Do they play football?
  4 Do they like Coca-Cola?
  5 Do they live near the centre of town?
  6 Do they drink beer?
  7 Do they work in a bank?

9 1 do 2 is / is 3 Are 4 do
  5 are 6 Do / do 7 Is / is 8 do

10 2 I'm 3 are 4 from 5 live
  6 do 7 from 8 I'm 9 but 10 in
  11 your 12 don't 13 a 14 job
  15 work 16 Do

11 2 P 3 P 4 S 5 S 6 S 7 P

13 A French B English, Spanish
  C Japanese, Portuguese
  D Brazilian, Italian

14 2 English 3 French 4 Italian
  5 Japanese 6 Spanish 7 German

16
twenty-three	23	sixty-four	64
thirty-seven	37	seventy-nine	79
forty-eight	48	eighty-six	86
fifty-one	51	ninety-two	92
fifty-five	55		

17
17p	seventeen p
£2.99	two pounds ninety-nine
58p	fifty-eight p
5p	five p
£26.47	twenty-six pounds forty-seven
£15.55	fifteen pounds fifty-five
75p	seventy-five p
£6.49	six pounds forty-nine
43p	forty three p
£99	ninety-nine pounds
£1.68	one pound sixty-eight
60p	sixty p
£5.72	five pounds seventy-two
£3.81	three pounds eighty-one
98p	ninety-eight p

18 2 59p 3 £49.99 4 84p 5 £28.10
  6 £62.45 7 50p 8 £19.23

19 2 £87.50 3 £11.30 4 £3.65
  5 £1.95 6 £99.99 7 80p 8 £32.49

Unit 6

1 2 It's eight fifteen. 3 It's ten thirty.
  4 It's four forty-five. 5 It's five fifteen.
  6 It's six thirty. 7 It's seven fifteen.
  8 It's nine o'clock.

2 2 11.00 3 10.30 4 4.45
  5 1.15 6 3.45

4 2 has 3 leaves / eight thirty 4 goes
  5 has 6 gets / six o'clock 7 goes

5 2 Marta never goes to work by bus.
  3 She usually has a sandwich in her office.
  4 She usually leaves work at 5.30.
  5 She never works in the evening.
  6 She sometimes goes to a restaurant in the evening.

7 2 Where does Angeles live?
  3 Does she have breakfast?
  4 When does she go to the concert hall?
  5 Where does she usually have lunch?
  6 What does she sometimes do in the afternoon?
  7 What time does she have dinner?
  8 Does she usually go out in the evening with friends?

8 2 She lives in a flat in Manhattan.
  3 No, she doesn't.
  4 She goes to the concert hall at nine o'clock.
  5 She usually has lunch at home.
  6 She sometimes goes for a walk in Central Park, and then listens to music.
  7 At six o'clock.
  8 Yes, she does.

9 2 doesn't live 3 doesn't have
  4 doesn't have 5 doesn't drink
  6 doesn't listen

10 2 Shinji doesn't leave work at one forty-five.
  3 Raoul doesn't go to work by taxi.
  4 Ramiro doesn't eat toast for breakfast.
  5 Piet doesn't get home at four thirty.
  6 Oliver doesn't speak French.
  7 Lidia doesn't work in a bank.
  8 Raquel doesn't have three children.

11 **Rosa**
  2 Does Rosa go to work by car?
    No, she doesn't.
  3 Does Rosa drink wine?
    Yes, she does.
  4 Does Rosa speak English?
    Yes, she does.

Paolo

2 Does Paolo go to work by car?
Yes, he does.
3 Does Paolo drink wine?
No, he doesn't.
4 Does Paolo speak English?
No, he doesn't.

12 2 don't 3 Do / don't 4 Do / do
5 Does / does 6 doesn't 7 doesn't

14 **See p93**

15 2 She leaves work. 3 She goes to bed.
4 She gets up. 5 She has lunch.
6 She has dinner.

17 2 Friday 3 Tuesday 4 Thursday
5 Sunday 6 Wednesday 7 Saturday

18 Monday, Tuesday, Wednesday, Thursday,
Friday, Saturday

19 2 at 3 on 4 at 5 in 6 On
7 In 8 At 9 in

Unit 7

1 you   *you*
he   *him*
she   *her*
it   *it*
we   *us*
they   *them*

2 2 her 3 them 4 me 5 us 6 you

3 2 them 3 him 4 it 5 us 6 you

4 3 What's that?
It's a house.
4 What's this?
It's a glass.
5 What's that?
It's a computer.
6 What's that?
It's a car.
7 What's this?
It's an ice-cream.
8 What's this?
It's a camera.
9 What's that?
It's a taxi.

5 3 This is a dictionary.
4 That's a sandwich.
5 That's a TV.
6 This is a pizza.
7 That's a bag.

6 2 a 3 h 4 c 5 i 6 f
7 g 8 d 9 b

7 2 How much is that dictionary?
Answer: d
3 What time do you start work?
Answer: g
4 How does Pierre go to work?
Answer: a
5 How many sports do you play?
Answer: b
6 Why does Sandra walk to school?
Answer: i
7 Where does Maria live?
Answer: h
8 Who is your favourite pop star?
Answer: c
9 How old are you?
Answer: f

9 2 e 3 c 4 b 5 a

10 2 Hawaii
3 is
4 wife number five
5 never
6 likes
7 seven

11 2 hot 3 old 4 new 5 big
6 small 7 expensive 8 cheap
9 horrible 10 lovely

12 2 Pilar's coffee is hot.
3 Alberto's car is old.
4 Sarah's car is new.
5 Alain's apple is big.
6 Judit's apple is small.
7 Maurice's computer is expensive.
8 Yumi's computer is cheap.
9 Keith's hamburger is horrible.
10 Catherine's hamburger is lovely.

15 2 The buildings in San Francisco aren't
very old.
3 The food is fantastic.
4 The food is cheap.
5 The hotel is very modern.
6 The hotel is cheap, but it isn't
comfortable.

7 The weather is very hot.
8 They go to the beach every day.

16 2 c 3 b 4 d 5 a

17 2 Can I have a ticket to London, please?
Here's your ticket and £5 change.
3 Can I send an email, please?
How much is it?
4 Can I help you?
How much is it?
5 Can I have a pizza, please?
£2.30.

Unit 8

1 2 bathroom
3 toilet
4 dining room
5 kitchen
6 bedroom

2 **B** toilet
C bathroom
D living room
E dining room
F kitchen

3 2 magazine 3 lamp 4 picture
5 shower 6 TV 7 sofa
8 CD player 9 armchair
10 video recorder 11 table
12 cooker

4 Sample answers
3 There's a telephone in the living room.
4 There are four chairs in the dining
room.
5 There's a TV in the bedroom.
6 There are two pictures in the dining
room.
7 There's a magazine in the bedroom.
8 There are two lamps in the bedroom.

5 3 No, there isn't.
4 No, there aren't.
5 Yes, there is.
6 No, there aren't.
7 No, there isn't.
8 Yes, there are.

6 3 Is there a magazine in the living room?
No, there isn't.
4 Are there any pictures in the dining room?
Yes, there are.
5 Is there a picture in the toilet?
Yes, there is.
6 Is there a TV in the bathroom?
No, there isn't.
7 Are there any CDs in the bedroom?
No, there aren't.
8 Is there a table in the dining room?
Yes, there is.

7 2 d 3 e 4 f 5 a 6 c

9 A armchair, lovely, never
B because, Japan, until
C dictionary, holiday, horrible, languages
D computer, delicious, expensive, fantastic
E afternoon, magazine, Portuguese

10 2 in 3 on 4 next to

11 2 on 3 in 4 under 5 on / next to
6 on / under

12 See p93

13 2 There are two.
3 Yes, there is.
4 They sit in the living room and watch
television or listen to music.
5 On the walls in the dining room.
6 No, it isn't. It's new.
7 They have lunch in the dining room.
8 Yes, there is.
9 Yes, they're very happy.

16 See p94

17 2 City Hotel
3 newsagent
4 post office
5 church

18 Sample answers
2 Yes, go down Park Street. Turn right into
London Road. Go past the Internet
Café. The supermarket is on the right.
3 Yes, go down Church Street. Turn
right into Oxford Road. Then turn left
at the City Hotel into Queen Street.
The bank is on the left.
4 Yes, go down Station Road, past Park
Street and Oxford Road. Turn right
into King's Road. The cinema is on
the left, next to the newsagent.

Unit 9

1 2 two thousand
3 nineteen ninety-nine
4 eighteen forty-eight
5 two thousand and two
6 nineteen eighty-seven
7 eighteen fifteen
8 two thousand and twenty
9 nineteen forty-five

2 2 1976
3 1588
4 1914
5 2003
6 1750
7 1862
8 1995

3 Maria 1930
Sofia 1957
Roberto 1955
Antonella 1959
Marco 1960
Luigi 1957
Rosa 1959
Alessandro 1978
Francesca 1980
Arianna 1985
Donatella 1985

4 2 When was Alessandro born?
He was born in 1978.
3 When were Arianna and Donatella
born?
They were born in 1985.
4 When were Antonella and Rosa born?
They were born in 1959.
5 When was Roberto born?
He was born in 1955.
6 When was Marco born?
He was born in 1960.
7 When were Sofia and Luigi born?
They were born in 1957.
8 When was Francesca born?
She was born in 1980.
9 When were Alberto and Maria born?
They were born in 1930.

6 2 was born 3 1564 4 was
5 were 6 was born 7 were born

7 Wolfgang Amadeus Mozart was a
musician. He was born in Salzburg,
Austria, in 1756. His wife's name was
Constanze and his children's names
were Carl and Franz. Carl was born in
1784 and Franz was born in 1791.

8 2 Was Amy Johnson English?
Yes, she was.
3 Was she born in Liverpool?
No, she wasn't. She was born in Hull.
4 Was she born in 1913?
No, she wasn't. She was born in 1903.
5 Was her husband's name Jim Mollison?
Yes, it was.

9 2 Charles Dickens wasn't a musician.
He was a writer.
3 Agatha Christie wasn't from Scotland.
She was from England.
4 Bill Clinton wasn't President of
Canada. He was President of the USA.
5 Marie Curie wasn't French. She was
Polish.
6 Laurel and Hardy weren't Australian.
They were American.
7 Humphry Bogart and Ingrid Bergman
weren't singers. They were actors.

10 2 Was / wasn't 3 weren't / were
4 were / was 5 Were / weren't
6 Was / wasn't / was

11 2 were 3 bought 4 went
5 said 6 saw 7 took

12 2 saw 3 were 4 went 5 bought
6 said 7 took 8 saw 9 was

14 **Food & drink:** wine, tea
Jobs: nurse, teacher, businessman
Rooms: dining room, kitchen,
bathroom
Places: bank, post office, railway station
Family: daughter, husband, parents
Days of the week: Sunday, Thursday,
Wednesday
Furniture: armchair, bed, table
Verbs: watch, listen, play
Adjectives: big, horrible, old

15 2 July
3 April
4 December
5 October
6 February
7 September
8 June
9 August
10 March
11 November
12 May

16 February
March
April
May
June
July
August
September
October
November
December

17 2nd second
3rd third
4th fourth
5th fifth
6th sixth
7th seventh
8th eighth
9th ninth
10th tenth
11th eleventh
12th twelfth
13th thirteenth
14th fourteenth
15th fifteenth

18 2 July 15th
3 March 22nd
4 November 12th
5 February 28th
6 June 5th
7 September 11th
8 December 31st
9 April 6th
10 August 19th
11 May 17th
12 October 10th
13 March 1st

Unit 10

1 2 cooked   3 stayed   4 worked
5 listened   6 watched

2 A cooked, worked, watched
B stayed, listened

3 2 listened   3 watched   4 cooked
5 worked   6 played

4 See p94

5 2 had   3 went   4 bought   5 ate   6 saw

6 a 4   b 8   c 1   d 6   e 7
f 2   g 9   h 3   i 5

7 2 ✓   3 ✗   4 ✓   5 ✓   6 ✗

9 3 Did he play football?
No, he didn't.
4 Did he buy a newspaper?
Yes, he did.
5 Did he do a lot of homework?
No, he didn't.
6 Did he watch television?
Yes, he did.
7 Did he go to work?
No, he didn't.
8 Did he listen to the radio?
Yes, he did.

10 2 Who did you see last weekend?
3 What time did you get home
yesterday evening?
4 How much homework did you do last
week?
5 What did you have for breakfast this
morning?
6 Where did you have lunch yesterday?

12 2 We didn't see our friends yesterday.
3 They didn't get up late yesterday morning.
4 You didn't play tennis.
5 I didn't have a big breakfast.
6 He didn't do a lot of housework at the
weekend.
7 We didn't watch a film on TV
yesterday evening.
8 Last week I didn't stay in a hotel in Paris.

14 2 play golf   3 go windsurfing   4 go
sailing   5 go walking   6 go dancing
7 go ice-skating   8 play baseball
9 play football   10 play cards   11 play
ice-hockey   12 go skiing

15 2 They had a really good time.
3 They stayed in a house with their
friends, Graham and Rachel.
4 Every morning they got up at nine
o'clock.
5 The weather was lovely – hot and sunny.
6 Hannah and Rachel usually played
tennis in the afternoon.
7 In the evening they cooked a big meal
in the house.
8 After dinner they went dancing.

16 See p95

Unit 11

1 2 ride a horse   3 use a computer
4 drive a car   5 draw   6 play the guitar
7 run   8 speak French   9 play the piano

3 3 Bill can use a computer.
4 Bill can't ride a horse.
5 Amanda can't read music.
6 Amanda can ride a horse.
7 Jill and Sam can read music.
8 Jill and Sam can use a computer.
9 Jill and Sam can't ride a horse.

4 3 Can Bill read music?
Yes, he can.
4 Can Bill ride a horse?
No, he can't.
5 Can Amanda use a computer?
No, she can't.
6 Can Amanda ride a horse?
Yes, she can.
7 Can Jill and Sam read music?
Yes, they can.
8 Can Jill and Sam use a computer?
Yes, they can.
9 Can Jill and Sam ride a horse?
No, they can't.

6 2 can   3 can   4 can't   5 France
6 can't   7 can   8 can   9 can't

8 2 C   3 A   4 B   5 C   6 A   7 B

9 2 Can I help you?
3 Can you tell me the time, please?
4 Can I have a pizza, please?
5 Can you speak more slowly, please?

10 2 Yes, I want to buy this newspaper.
3 It's about ten forty-five.
4 Yes, of course. Small, medium, or large?
5 I'm sorry. Can you understand now?

12 2 December   3 football   4 Tuesday
5 weekend   6 bought   7 garden

13 2 A I can't find my plane ticket.
B You put it on the table.
3 A I don't understand this word.
B Check it in your dictionary.
4 A This computer doesn't work.
B Did you push this button?
5 A I'm lost. Can you help me?
B Where do you want to go?
6 A What's the matter?
B The CD player's broken.

Unit 12

1
2 I'd like to use your dictionary
3 I'd like to buy her new CD.
4 I'd like a stamp.
5 I'd like to see the new Stephen Spielberg film.
6 I'd like to be a student again!

2
3 I'd like a glass of water, please.
4 I'd like to play chess, please.
5 I'd like to listen to a CD, please.
6 I'd like a stamp, please.
7 I'd like a cup of coffee, please.
8 I'd like to buy a computer, please.

3
3 Would you like to watch a video?
4 Would you like a glass of orange juice?
5 Would you like some cake?
6 Would you like to go skiing?
7 Would you like a pizza?
8 Would you like to play a computer game?

4
2 chicken
3 fish
4 fries
5 fruit
6 mineral water
7 salad
8 soup
9 tomato
10 vegetables

5
2 Yes, er, I'd like the soup to start, please.
3 And what would you like for your main course?
4 Can I have the fish, please?
5 The fish. Very good. And what would you like to drink?
6 Can I have a glass of white wine, please?
7 Certainly. A glass of white wine.
8 And I'd like a bottle of mineral water, too.
9 Yes, of course. Thank you.

6 tomato soup, roast chicken and salad, fries, apple pie and cream, beer, coffee

7
2 What would you like to start?
3 And for your main course?
4 How would you like it cooked?
5 Can I have the roast chicken
6 I'd like a glass of white wine

9
2 day 3 new 4 sister 5 my
6 shop 7 usually

11
2 Mitsuo
3 Helga
4 Serena
5 Helga and Mitsuo
6 Jake
7 Serena
8 Mitsuo

12
2 In a newsagent
3 In the street
4 In a clothes shop
5 At the market
6 In a newsagent

13
1 Next to
2 No, thanks
3 in a size 44
4 try on / The changing rooms
5 two kilos of / that's all
6 Do you sell

Unit 13

1
2 red 3 white 4 green 5 brown
6 black 7 blue 8 grey

2
4 studying 5 running 6 making
7 sitting 8 watching 9 phoning
10 eating

3
2 I'm learning English.
3 We're sitting in the living room.
4 She's talking to her sister.
5 They're enjoying the film.
6 He's dancing.
7 I'm working at home.

4
2 they aren't drinking / They're drinking
3 he isn't sitting / He's sitting
4 I'm not having / I'm having
5 she isn't walking / She's running
6 you aren't wearing / You're wearing

5
3 Is Elena reading a book?
   No, she isn't. She's listening to music.
4 Are Pascal and Paul wearing T-shirts?
   Yes, they are.
5 Is Roberto sitting on the beach?
   Yes, he is.
6 Are Roberto and Elena swimming?
   No, they aren't. Roberto is reading and Elena is listening to music.

7 Is Elena drinking Coca-Cola?
   Yes, she is.
8 Is Roberto reading a magazine?
   No, he isn't. He's reading a book.

6
2 are / 'm 3 Does 4 do 5 is
6 Does / does

7
2 aren't 3 isn't 4 don't 5 'm not
6 doesn't

9
2 He's reading the newspaper.
3 The sun's shining and it's really hot.
4 They usually stay with their friends, Ana and Zé.
5 They're staying in a hotel.
6 They go swimming.

10
2 trousers 3 shorts 4 coat
5 trainers 6 jumper 7 dress
8 skirt 9 sandals 10 shirt
11 shoes 12 jacket 13 hat

11
2 b 3 c 4 b 5 d 6 a 7 c 8 d

12 Sample answers
1 Mike's wearing a jacket, a shirt, trousers, and shoes.
2 Carol's wearing a hat, coat, jumper, skirt, and boots.

14
2 hot 3 hungry 4 cold
5 thirsty 6 bored

15
2 a 3 f 4 b 5 e 6 c

Unit 14

1
2 On Monday evening he's going to the cinema with Jane.
3 On Tuesday morning he's seeing the dentist.
4 On Tuesday afternoon he's playing football.
5 On Wednesday morning he's driving to Liverpool.
6 On Wednesday afternoon he's visiting Uncle Joseph.

2
3 F 4 P 5 F 6 P 7 P 8 F

3
2 How's she travelling?
   She's travelling by train.
3 Who's she meeting?
   She's meeting Sophie.
4 Where's she meeting her?
   She's meeting her at Paddington Station.

5 When's she going to Cambridge?
  She's going to Cambridge at one
  o'clock.
6 Why's she going to Cambridge?
  She's going to Cambridge to see Mike.
7 What's she doing on Friday evening?
  She's going to bed early.

4 Sample answers
  Monday: 8.00 p.m. – go for a meal with
  Pete
  Tuesday: 8.30 p.m. – meet Lisa and
  Mark at the cinema
  Wednesday: 2.00 p.m. – see the dentist
  Thursday: 2.00 p.m. – play tennis with
  Jack
  Friday: Go to London – meet Tina at
  the station at 9.30

6 The stressed words are underlined.
  1 'What's your job?'
    'I'm a doctor. What's your job?'

2 'What would you like?'
  'A coffee. What would you like?'
3 'Where do you work?'
  'In Rome. Where do you work?'
4 'Where are you from?'
  'Prague. Where are you from?'

8 2 underground 3 ship 4 bicycle

9 2 packed
  3 collected
  4 caught
  5 arrived
  6 went
  7 had

10 a 6 b 2 c 5 d 3 e 1 f 4

11 2 They left their car in a street near a
    canal.
  3 They stayed in Amsterdam for five days.
  4 No, they didn't.
  5 They caught the plane.
  6 The police found their car a week later.

12 2 a 3 b 4 c

13 **Zoo**
   Prince Charles Park
   Open from *10.00* to *4.00*
   Adults £8 Children £4

   Science Museum
   Open from *9.30* to *6.00* every day.
   Adults £5 Children £3

   Bus Tour of the City
   The bus leaves at 9.00, 11.00,
   1.00 and 3.00 from Queen Street.
   The tour takes *two* hours.

Unit 6 14

1 H	O	2 S	P	I	3 T	A	L		
		P			E				
		A		4 E	A	T	S		
5 W	I	N	E					6 F	
		I		7 S		8 C	A	R	
		S		O				I	
	9 P	H	O	N	10 E			D	
	I				L			11 A	M
	Z		12 T	W	E	N	13 T	Y	
	Z				V		I		
14 T	A	X	I		E		15 M	Y	
				16 A	N		E		

Unit 8 12

Unit 8 16

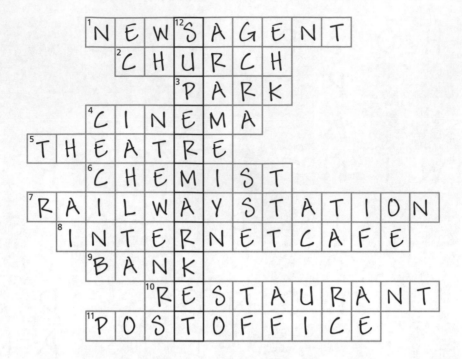

```
¹N E W ¹²S A G E N T
   ²C H U R C H
      ³P A R K
   ⁴C I N E M A
⁵T H E A T R E
   ⁶C H E M I S T
⁷R A I L W A Y S T A T I O N
  ⁸I N T E R N E T C A F E
   ⁹B A N K
      ¹⁰R E S T A U R A N T
¹¹P O S T O F F I C E
```

Unit 10 4

S	A	D	G	D	T	A
A	N	F	O	U	G	T
W	E	N	T	N	E	A
E	B	O	U	G	H	T
N	F	W	P	U	A	E
K	A	T	P	S	D	M

arena
Sports Centre

APPLICATION FORM

Mr ✓　　Mrs ☐　　Miss ☐　　Ms ☐　(please tick)

Full name	Boris Wehr
Address	26, London Road
	Oxford
Postcode	OX3 8EF
Phone number	01865 926841
Date of birth	1st February, 1985
Nationality	German

What sports are you interested in? (please circle)

swimming　(squash)　(fitness training)
basketball　athletics　tennis

Phonetic symbols

Consonants

1	/p/	as in	**pen**	/pen/
2	/b/	as in	**big**	/bɪg/
3	/t/	as in	**tea**	/tiː/
4	/d/	as in	**do**	/duː/
5	/k/	as in	**cat**	/kæt/
6	/g/	as in	**go**	/gəʊ/
7	/f/	as in	**four**	/fɔː/
8	/v/	as in	**very**	/ˈveri/
9	/s/	as in	**son**	/sʌn/
10	/z/	as in	**zoo**	/zuː/
11	/l/	as in	**live**	/lɪv/
12	/m/	as in	**my**	/maɪ/
13	/n/	as in	**near**	/nɪə/
14	/h/	as in	**happy**	/ˈhæpi/
15	/r/	as in	**red**	/red/
16	/j/	as in	**yes**	/jes/
17	/w/	as in	**want**	/wɒnt/
18	/θ/	as in	**thanks**	/θæŋks/
19	/ð/	as in	**the**	/ðə/
20	/ʃ/	as in	**she**	/ʃiː/
21	/ʒ/	as in	**television**	/ˈtelɪvɪʒn/
22	/tʃ/	as in	**child**	/tʃaɪld/
23	/dʒ/	as in	**German**	/ˈdʒɜːmən/
24	/ŋ/	as in	**English**	/ˈɪŋglɪʃ/

Vowels

25	/iː/	as in	**see**	/siː/
26	/ɪ/	as in	**his**	/hɪz/
27	/i/	as in	**twenty**	/ˈtwenti/
28	/e/	as in	**ten**	/ten/
29	/æ/	as in	**stamp**	/stæmp/
30	/ɑː/	as in	**father**	/ˈfɑːðə/
31	/ɒ/	as in	**hot**	/hɒt/
32	/ɔː/	as in	**morning**	/ˈmɔːnɪŋ/
33	/ʊ/	as in	**football**	/ˈfʊtbɔːl/
34	/uː/	as in	**you**	/juː/
35	/ʌ/	as in	**sun**	/sʌn/
36	/ɜː/	as in	**learn**	/lɜːn/
37	/ə/	as in	**letter**	/ˈletə/

Diphthongs (two vowels together)

38	/eɪ/	as in	**name**	/neɪm/
39	/əʊ/	as in	**no**	/nəʊ/
40	/aɪ/	as in	**my**	/maɪ/
41	/aʊ/	as in	**how**	/haʊ/
42	/ɔɪ/	as in	**boy**	/bɔɪ/
43	/ɪə/	as in	**hear**	/hɪə/
44	/eə/	as in	**where**	/weə/
45	/ʊə/	as in	**tour**	/tʊə/